OUTDOOR DECOR

Decorative Projects for the Porch, Patio & Yard

The Home Decorating Institute®

Copyright © 1996 Creative Publishing international, Inc.
5900 Green Oak Drive Minnetonka, Minnesota 55343 • 1-800-328-3895 • All rights reserved • Printed in U.S.A.

Library of Congress Cataloging-in-Publication Data Outdoor decor: decorative projects for the porch, patio & yard/the Home Decorating Institute.
p. cm. — (Arts & crafts for home decorating) Includes index. ISBN 0-86573-385-6 (hardcover) ISBN 0-86573-386-4 (softcover) 1. Garden ornaments
and furniture. I. Home Decorating Institute (Minnetonka, Minn.) II. Series.   SB473.5.D435 1996 712'.6 — dc20   95-20876 CIP

CONTENTS

Decorating the Outdoors

The Yard & Garden

The Porch
& Patio

Creative
Lighting Effects

DECORATING THE OUTDOORS

*Enhance the natural surroundings
with outdoor accessories
for the front entrance,
patio, and garden.*

Accessories can beautify the front entrance of your home, brighten a porch or patio, and add charm to the garden and yard. Personalize your outdoor living space with handcrafted items from fabric and wood. You can even supplement the sights and sounds of nature with a tiered water fountain constructed from terra-cotta and wind chimes made from old silverware.

Add color with the abundant use of flowers in container gardens and hanging baskets. Plant flowers in planter boxes made to perfectly fit the railing of your deck. Build your own customized trellises, or create a water garden filled with aquatic plants.

Make the patio and backyard more comfortable and inviting, using softly padded cushions for the outdoor furniture with a coordinating tablecloth and hammock. And welcome wild birds to the yard with handmade birdhouses and decorative feeders.

For added drama in the evenings, use string lights to accent an arbor or a floodlight to highlight a tree or unique garden statue. And line a walking path with luminaries.

Decorative post with a finial *is positioned at the entrance to a home. Shown here as a signpost for a street address, a decorative post can also be used for hanging plants, a banner, or a wind sock as on page 61.*

Potted plants *are a traditional approach to decorating front entrances. Left, several container gardens (page 16) are grouped together for impact, and a hanging basket (page 28) flanks the doorway.*

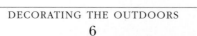

DECORATING THE FRONT ENTRANCE

$\mathbf{M}$ake a statement at the front entrance of your home with a few decorative elements. For a traditional approach, use container gardens near the front door, using either a single variety of flowers or a mix of several. Or try a more personalized accessory, such as the decorative signpost for a street address shown here. For an attention-getting evening display, use luminaries to highlight the front entrance.

Luminaries (right) can be used to line the driveway or create a display at the front door. These creative luminaries are actually minnow buckets with pillar candles placed inside.

Wreath (below) is hung on a fence to create an eye-catching display where least expected.

DECORATING THE YARD & GARDEN

A beautiful yard and garden can be a soothing environment. An abundance of plantings can help at varied heights, some climbing on trellises with others suspended in hanging baskets. To vary the elements in the garden, add a few complementary accessories.

In the backyard, a hammock hung between two trees creates a feeling of leisure and a tree table becomes a resting place for a favorite book. A decorative birdhouse and perhaps a bird feeder or two can accessorize the yard and encourage songbirds to visit.

Evergreen (left) is decorated with string lights to add drama to a backyard garden.

Backyard (opposite) is an inviting setting. A hammock (page 68) is hung between two tall shade trees, ready for a carefree escape. The tree table (page 93) is the perfect place to set a cool drink. The painted birdhouse (page 42) adds the finishing touch.

Tranquil retreat (below) is created in a corner of the backyard. A water garden (page 36) with a wooden surround sits near a garden bench. For comfort, the bench has been cushioned with a soft pad (page 88).

DECORATING THE PORCH & PATIO

A porch or patio, surrounded by nature, is the perfect setting for gatherings of family and friends—or for you to relax quietly with a tall glass of lemonade.

Container gardens created in deck rail planters and floor pots can soften and beautify an otherwise hard-surfaced deck or patio of wood, brick, or concrete. To create a more inviting space, add soft cushions, pretty table appointments, and perhaps a wind chime or water fountain.

Tablecloth (opposite), designed for an umbrella-style table (page 74), helps create a festive dining atmosphere.

Wind chimes (right), cleverly made from old silverware as on page 104, are suspended over the patio from the eaves.

Cushions (below) add comfort to patio chairs. Customize the cushions to your furniture as on page 82.

SEASONAL DECORATING

Vary your outdoor decorating with the change of the seasons, to give your surroundings a fresh, new look. Choose accessories that complement the ever-changing displays of nature, or create a display that contrasts boldly.

Spring wind sock and banner *(left) are displayed from decorative garden posts (page 60).*

Autumn deck rail planter *(below) contains a variety of colorful annuals. Make the planter as on pages 24 to 27.*

Summer birdhouses *(above) are both decorative and functional. Make the birdhouses as on pages 42 to 45.*

Winter holiday display *(left) includes luminaries from ice (page 120) and arborvitae embellished with string lights (page 114).*

The Yard & Garden

CONTAINER GARDENS

Create an instant flower garden anywhere you can place a pot or hang a basket. Although container gardening is most often used for annuals, any plant varieties can be grown in containers, provided the container is of a suitable size for the plants and the containers are placed in an area that has the correct lighting conditions. If perennials or roses are planted in containers, they must be wintered in the ground if you live in a cold climate. Otherwise, the soil in the containers will repeatedly freeze and thaw, killing the plants.

Containers with drainage holes are preferred. For pottery crocks and other containers without drainage, you can use an inner container with drainage holes for the plants, and place it inside the decorative container. Because metal containers and dark plastic containers may become quite hot, you may want to use a small inner container for the plants and insulate the space between the two containers with landscape bark.

It is important that you use a potting mix, rather than soil, because the plants are confined to a small space and the roots cannot reach far for nutrients. A good porous mix that holds moisture consists of equal parts of garden soil, compost or peat moss, and vermiculite; the vermiculite holds up to twenty times its weight in moisture. If the plant varieties you have chosen require dry roots, substitute sand or perlite for the vermiculite.

Commercial potting mixes are also available, including soil-based and soilless mixes. Soilless potting mix is lightweight, making it a good choice for window boxes and hanging planters that could become too heavy to install and for large containers that you may want to relocate.

Because container gardens tend to dry out, they need to be watered frequently. If you are watering with a hose, use a wand to prevent dislodging the soil in the container. Regular feeding with a water-soluble fertilizer is important to replace the soil nutrients. At weekly intervals, add 1 tablespoon (15 mL) of fertilizer per gallon (3.8 L) of water when you are watering the container garden. Or each time you water the plants, add a pinch of the fertilizer to the water.

- Container; saucer, if container is placed on deck or patio, to protect surface from water damage due to drainage.
- Commercial potting mix or mixture of equal parts of garden soil, compost or peat moss, and vermiculite;

substitute sand or perlite for the vermiculite if the plants need dry roots.
- Rocks, gravel, pottery shards, or Styrofoam® beads.
- Sheet moss or mulch, optional.

HOW TO PLANT A CONTAINER GARDEN

1 Place a piece of broken pottery in the bottom of the container, placing it so it arches over drainage hole; this helps prevent hole from becoming clogged with soil. Add 1" to 2" (2.5 to 6.5 cm) layer of rocks, gravel, pottery shards, or Styrofoam beads.

2 Fill the container partially with potting mix. Test-fit the plants while they are still in their containers to determine desired arrangement and spacing.

3 Arrange the plants, surrounding them with potting mix; the root balls of the plants should be ½" to 1" (1.3 to 2.5 cm) below the rim of container. Fill in remaining space with potting mix. Press potting mix gently in place with your hands, to eliminate air pockets.

4 Cover potting mix with sheet moss or mulch, if desired; this helps soil retain moisture. Water the plants thoroughly. Place container in shade for a few days, to help plants recover from the shock of transplanting.

SETTINGS FOR CONTAINER GARDENS

Container gardens are so portable and versatile that they can be located virtually anywhere, even in unexpected areas. To create an appealing setting, give some thought to the placement of the containers. An ordinary concrete patio can become a picturesque environment with container gardening. Or a basic privacy fence can come alive with foliage in hanging baskets.

When planning a container garden, group several containers together for greater impact. To create a multilevel garden, take advantage of existing stairs or use pedestals and benches to display plantings. For depth, stagger the placement of the containers rather than align them in a straight row.

Impressive grouping of potted plants
(below) lines the front walkway to a house,
and a hanging basket of colorful bougainvillea
greets guests at the door.

Hollowed-out log (above) is used for a container garden, creating a
refreshing oasis on a backyard lawn.

Moss-lined baskets with impatiens (opposite) decorate a
privacy fence.

Containers of annuals (opposite) are interspersed among
the perennials in a flower bed. The containers can be
moved to new locations as various perennials come
into bloom.

**Patio
garden**
consists
of con-
tainers in
various sizes
and shapes.
Contrasting with
the hard surface
of the patio, the
garden enlivens
and softens
the area.

CREATIVE CONTAINERS

To personalize container gardens, use nontraditional containers rather than the standard planters and pots found in garden centers. For old-fashioned, rustic appeal, consider using quaint found items, such as tin watering cans, old wheelbarrows, and wooden crates. Or create a fanciful, picturesque patio garden, using a collection of pretty teapots. The choice of containers is unlimited.

Depending on the found items you choose, you may want to plant directly into the containers or simply insert prepotted plants. Some items, including old colanders and wire baskets, provide the proper drainage for plants, while others may require a layer of pebbles at the bottom of the container to protect the plant's root system from water damage.

Pair of teapots (above), *used as flowerpots, are arranged on a patio table.*

Grapevine wreaths, stacked around a plastic ice cream bucket, create a container with a woodsy look. Tuck moss into the wreaths for added texture.

Fishing creel (above) stuffed with flowerpots hangs on a porch wall.

Cowboy boots (right) are used as holders for a cactus and other potted plants.

Old wagon and sprinkling can (below) are filled with plants and grouped together for a clever garden setting.

(Continued)

CREATIVE CONTAINERS (CONTINUED)

Colander *hung from a tree branch contains petunias and variegated vinca plants.*

Picnic basket, *filled with favorite annuals, becomes a unique container. Plant flowers in flowerpots, and insert a dish in the bottom of the basket to collect any water seepage from drainage holes.*

Hanging mailbox near the back door holds small pots of flowers, including marigolds, violas, and lobelia.

Cheese boxes and wooden crates (below) create a multilevel container garden.

DECK RAIL PLANTERS

Add a colorful display of flowers along the railing of your deck, arranging them in custom planter boxes. The deck rail planter, designed to hold potted plants, is basically a four-sided bottomless box with spacers on the underside that hold it snugly in place over the rail. The pots and saucers rest directly on the deck rail. Made from cedar, the box may be constructed with the rough side of the boards facing out. Or, for a more refined finish on a painted box, use the smooth side of the boards facing out.

The planter can be custom-built to any length and has an outside width of 10" (25.5 cm). The inside width of the planter is 8½" (21.8 cm), and, when the planter box is placed over the rail, the inside height is 6¼" (15.7 cm); select plant containers that fit these inside dimensions. For planter boxes longer than 32" (81.5 cm),

add a center support, securing it to the front and back of the box. The center support prevents the box from warping.

Determine the desired length of the planter box; if you are planning to use specific sizes of pots and saucers in the box, keep in mind that the inside length of the box will be 2" (5 cm) shorter than the outside length. For a long box with a center support, the inside length is 2¾" (7 cm) shorter than the outside length. It may be helpful to draw a sketch, including the pots that will be used in the box.

When determining the lumber required, allow extra length, in order to avoid the placement of knots at the ends of cut pieces. This will prevent difficulty when cutting the pieces and when inserting the screws.

MATERIALS

- 1 × 8 cedar lumber.
- 8 × 3" (7.5 cm) galvanized drywall screws, or deck screws.
- 6 × 1⅝" (4 cm) galvanized drywall screws, or deck screws.
- Exterior wood glue, such as Titebond® II.
- Razor knife.
- Jigsaw or circular saw.
- Drill and ⅛" drill bit.

Deck rail planter *is a simple bottomless box. Spacer blocks on the underside straddle the railing for a snug fit. The flowerpots and saucers rest directly on the deck rail.*

HOW TO MAKE A DECK RAIL PLANTER

1 Mark desired length of planter on face side of 1 × 8 lumber, for front piece. Lightly score on marked line, using a razor knife; this prevents wood from splintering when cut. Cut front piece, using a jigsaw. Mark and cut back piece to same length as front piece.

2 Mark 8½" (21.8 cm) length on lumber, for end piece; score with razor knife, and cut with jigsaw. Repeat to cut remaining end piece and, if necessary, the center support piece.

3 Mark a line on end piece, parallel to grain of wood, 1" (2.5 cm) from the lower edge; score with razor knife and cut with jigsaw on marked line. Repeat for the remaining end piece and for center support. Set aside 1" (2.5 cm) strips, to use for spacer blocks in step 7.

4 Mark placement for three screws, ¾" (2 cm) from one end of front piece, with one mark 1" (2.5 cm) from upper edge, one 2" (5 cm) from lower edge, and one centered between the two marks. Repeat at opposite end of front piece. If box has center support, also mark placement for row of screws at center of board. Mark back piece the same as front piece.

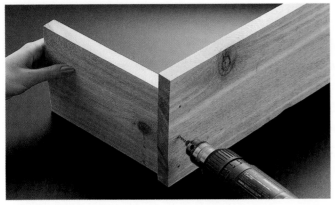

5 Stand end piece upright. Position front piece against end piece, extending it ¼" (6 mm) beyond end piece. Predrill holes for screws, using ⅛" drill bit; secure with 3" (7.5 cm) screws. Repeat for remaining end piece.

6 Position center support, if used, at center of front piece. Predrill holes, and secure screws. Secure back piece to end pieces and center support.

$$5 \tfrac{1}{2} \quad \text{WIDTH OF DECK RAIL}$$
$$+ \tfrac{1}{8}$$
$$\overline{5 \tfrac{5}{8}}$$

$$8 \tfrac{1}{2} \quad \text{INSIDE WIDTH OF BOX}$$
$$- 5 \tfrac{5}{8}$$
$$\overline{2 \tfrac{7}{8}}$$

$$2 \tfrac{7}{8} \div 2 = 1 \tfrac{7}{16}$$

7 Add ⅛" (3 mm) to width of deck rail; subtract this measurement from inside width of box. Cut spacer blocks from the 1" (2.5 cm) strips set aside in step 3, with length of each block equal to one-half this measurement. You will need two spacer blocks for each end piece and two for center support.

8 Glue spacer blocks to each side of end pieces and center support as shown, with the blocks offset ⅛" (3 mm) from the edges of front and end pieces; distance between the blocks is slightly wider than the deck rail. Predrill hole into each block, using ⅛" drill bit; secure blocks, using 1⅝" (4 cm) screws. Planter may be left unfinished or may be stained or painted as in step 9.

9 Apply exterior wood stain **(a)**, or apply exterior primer, with two coats of primer on ends of boards. Then apply exterior paint **(b).**

HANGING BASKETS

For a lush hanging basket overflowing with flowers, make an arrangement using a wire-frame basket. The flowers are planted not only at the top of the basket, but also at the sides for a fuller effect. The open framework of the wire basket allows the plants to be inserted at various levels, and, once mature, the plants will conceal the frame.

Wire baskets are available at garden centers in a variety of sizes, generally ranging from 8" to 20" (20.5 to 51 cm) in diameter. Although the baskets themselves are lightweight, once filled and well watered, hanging baskets can become quite heavy. Make sure the basket is suspended from a bracket or hook that is securely anchored. To reduce the weight, use a soilless planting mix.

Because hanging baskets need frequent watering, hang them in a convenient location. Add a plastic lining between the moss and the potting mix to help retain the moisture.

When selecting the plants for the hanging basket, choose a combination of bushy and trailing plants that complement each other. To maintain the arrangement, regularly trim off any dead flowers and leaves as well as any overvigorous plant growth.

MATERIALS

- Several plants in combination of bushy and trailing varieties.
- Wire basket.
- Sheet moss.
- Black plastic sheeting.
- Plastic wrap.
- Soilless potting mix.
- Wire plant hanger, or metal chains and S-hooks.
- Wall bracket or ceiling hook.

HOW TO MAKE A HANGING BASKET

1 Line wire basket with sheet moss, placing large piece in bottom of basket and tearing off smaller pieces to fit along sides; overlap pieces, and extend moss to the upper edge of basket.

2 Place plastic sheet inside the basket, over the moss; trim plastic about ¾" (2 cm) below upper edge of the basket. Cut small slashes in plastic near the base, for drainage. Where plants will be inserted, cut X-shaped slashes through plastic and moss, at various levels in lower half of basket. Fill basket with potting mix, up to the X-shaped slashes.

3 Secure wire plant hanger to basket, spacing wires evenly; wrap and twist ends securely. Or secure three lengths of metal chain to basket; secure ends of chain to S-hook.

4 Wrap a plant loosely with a sheet of plastic wrap; this allows you to easily insert the plant through the slash in the plastic and moss.

5 Insert foliage of the plant, from inside of basket, through the slash in plastic and moss. Remove plastic wrapping, and carefully spread the roots apart inside basket. Repeat for remaining slashes. Fill basket partway with potting mix, allowing space for the plants on the top of the basket.

6 Arrange the plants as desired on top of basket, distributing them evenly so the basket will hang level; surround plants with potting mix. Fill in any remaining space in basket with potting mix, leaving at least ½" (1.3 cm) of space at top for watering.

7 Fill in the spaces between the plants with moss; this helps hold moisture between waterings. Hang basket from wall bracket or ceiling hook. Water thoroughly.

TRELLISES

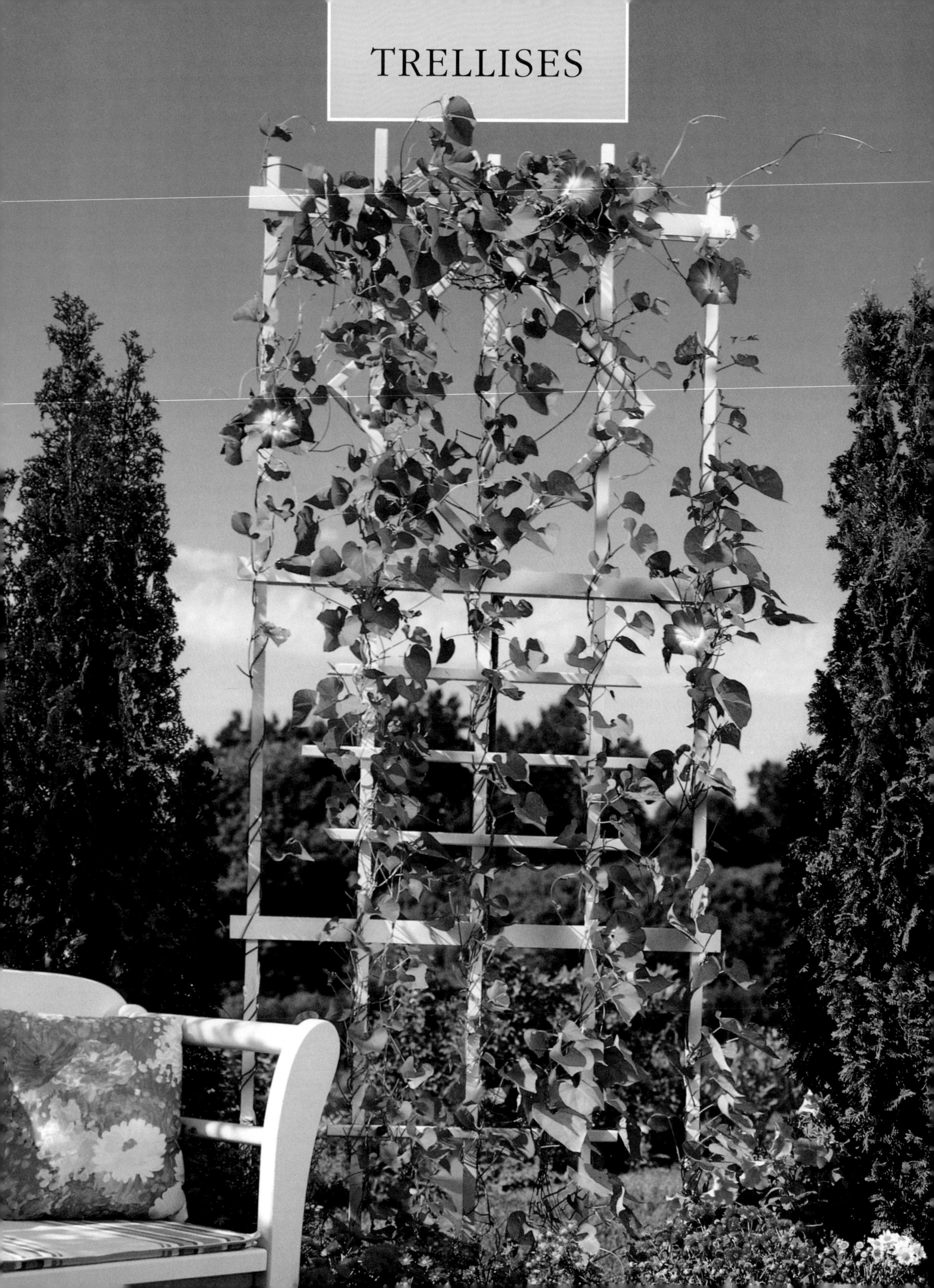

Trellises, with customized dimensions and detailing, are easy to make. Use trellises and climbing plants to add interest to a plain surface, such as a garage wall or fence. To create a nearly invisible plant support over a window, extend the trellis above the window, using monofilament fishing line.

More of a craft project than a woodworking project, trellises are made using parting stop, lath, and screen molding. Parting stop is used for the vertical legs of the trellis. Wider lath, sometimes called lattice, is used for the horizontal supports. A horizontal lath piece is secured to both the front and back of the trellis for all but the bottom horizontal support. Motifs, such as squares, diamonds, and arrows, are cut from screen molding and used to trim the trellis. Parting stop, lath, and screen molding are readily available at building supply stores.

When designing a trellis, take into consideration the space where it will be displayed and the anticipated height of the climbing plants that will be used with the trellis. For design interest, stagger the lengths of the vertical legs of the trellis. An odd number of legs is usually most attractive. Support tall trellises with three horizontal pieces of lath. Experiment, making sketches of possible designs until you find a pleasing arrangement. Trellis motifs can be customized to repeat a theme or design line found in surrounding pieces, such as furniture or fences.

For a subtle look, paint the trellis to match the surface it is placed against. Or paint the trellis in a contrasting color for a structure that makes a design statement year-round.

CLIMBING PLANTS

ANNUAL PLANTS

Asarina (Climbing Snapdragon)	Nasturtium	
Morning Glory	Scarlet Runner Bean	
	Sweet Pea	

PERENNIAL PLANTS

Clematis	Dutchman's Pipe
Climbing Hydrangea	Porcelainberry
Climbing Rose	Silver Lace Vine

MATERIALS

- ½" × ¾" (1.3 × 2 cm) pine parting stop, for vertical legs.
- ¼" × 1⅜" (6 mm × 3.5 cm) pine lath, for front and back horizontal supports.
- ¼" × ¾" (6 mm × 2 cm) pine or oak screen molding, for decorative embellishments.
- Drill and ⅟16" drill bit.
- Exterior wood glue.
- #19 × ½" (1.3 cm) wire brads.
- Miter box and backsaw.
- Monofilament fishing line, 30-lb. (13.5 k) test, for combination wood and string trellis.
- Exterior primer; exterior paint.

Trellises can be designed for a variety of spaces. Opposite, a free-standing trellis is supported with metal stakes. Right, a trellis is customized to fit under and around a window.

HOW TO MAKE A WOOD TRELLIS

1 Draw sketch of trellis to the desired dimensions; allow for 4" to 8" (10 to 20.5 cm) between each vertical leg. Finished width of trellis is equal to sum of distance between vertical legs plus ¾" (2 cm) for each vertical leg. Plan for horizontal supports to be positioned at the bottom, about 2" (5 cm) from top, and about two-thirds the distance from the bottom. Additional supports may be added, if desired.

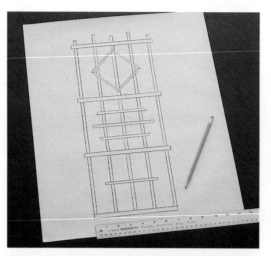

2 Mark and cut parting stop to desired length for each vertical leg; guide cuts, if desired, using miter box and 90° guide. For the horizontal supports on back side of trellis, cut pieces of lath with length equal to the finished width of trellis. Remaining horizontal supports for front of trellis are cut in step 5.

3 Place the vertical legs in desired arrangement, ¾" (2 cm) side up, on smooth, flat surface, with bottom of legs aligned. Place horizontal supports over legs as determined in step 1.

4 Glue and nail bottom horizontal support to legs, using two brads at each joint, and T-square or carpenter's square to ensure square corners; stagger placement of nails to help prevent splitting wood. Start at one side, and work toward the opposite side. Repeat to secure upper horizontal support, then middle supports.

5 Turn trellis over. Cut and position piece of lath over top and middle supports; lath can be cut to the width of trellis or with ends extending about 1" (2.5 cm) beyond legs. Secure each piece of lath with exterior wood glue and a brad at each vertical leg.

6 Cut pieces of screen molding as desired for embellishments, using tips on page 34. Position pieces, using glue. When the glue is tacky, secure with at least two brads; place scrap piece of lath under trellis for support when pounding brads.

7 Apply exterior primer to trellis; allow to dry. Paint as desired, using exterior paint. Mount trellis (page 34).

HOW TO MAKE A COMBINATION WOOD & STRING TRELLIS

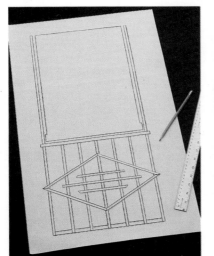

1 Determine the dimensions, and draw a sketch of the trellis, with the width at least 2" (5 cm) wider than width of window and upper edge of the top horizontal support just below lower edge of the window. Extend the outer legs to the desired height of the string portion of the trellis.

2 Cut the legs and the horizontal supports as in step 2, opposite. Arrange the trellis pieces as in step 3, opposite; position a horizontal support at bottom of the trellis and below the window. Mark the outer legs at upper edge of top horizontal support.

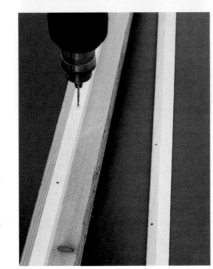

3 Mark holes for fishing line on ½" (1.3 cm) side of outer legs at 3" to 4" (7.5 to 10 cm) intervals, from marks to upper end. Drill at markings, using ¹⁄₁₆" drill bit.

4 Reposition outer legs, and assemble trellis as in steps 4 to 6, opposite. Mount trellis (page 34). Lace fishing line through drilled holes, starting at top of one leg and working from side to side as shown; cut the line, leaving excess at ends. Wrap fishing line around outer leg of trellis and tie in knot; pull line taut, and tie off remaining end.

TIPS FOR SCREEN MOLDING MOTIFS

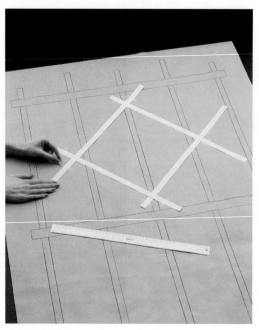

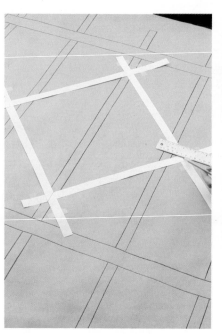

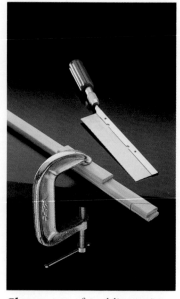

Experiment with strips of paper cut 3/4" (2 cm) wide to test the designs. Extend the ends of the design motifs beyond the legs of trellis when possible, to help prevent splitting the wood with brads.

Make paper patterns for diamonds, squares, and arrows, marking lines for miter cuts on both upper and lower pattern pieces. Cut patterns, and transfer markings to moldings.

Clamp sets of molding strips together to save time and ensure uniform lengths when making mitered cuts. Clamp pieces and make mitered cut at one end; repeat for mitered cut at opposite end.

HOW TO MOUNT A TRELLIS

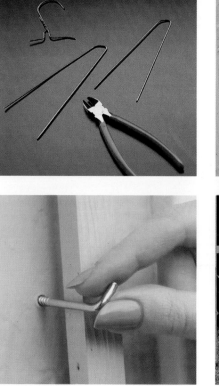

1 **Surface mount.** Cut clothes hanger, using wire cutter, to make two stakes as shown; discard the upper portion of hanger.

2 Position the trellis against a wall or a fence. Secure the bottom of trellis, using a coat-hanger stake at each end of the horizontal slat.

3 Secure the top of the trellis with a shoulder hook at each side; predrill the holes as necessary.

Freestanding mount. Insert metal stakes into the ground with distance between stakes equal to width of the trellis. Attach trellis to the stakes, using lengths of plastic-coated wire.

MORE IDEAS
FOR TRELLISES

Discarded window guard (above) provides a formal support for clematis.

Rustic trellis (left) is made using both straight and forked branches. Secure the branches with nails or wrapped wire. For branches that can be shaped, use freshly cut, green branches.

Trellis motifs (below) are painted to contrast with the trellis frame for a decorative effect.

WATER GARDENS

Turn a barrel planter or a vinyl tub into a tranquil water garden. Placed near a bench or table, water gardens add a unique focal point in a landscape.

Barrel planters are readily available at most lawn and garden stores. Depending on the type selected, it may be necessary to make the barrel watertight. Cypress, cedar, or redwood barrels with tongue-and-groove construction are self-sealing. Fill and replenish any of these barrels with water until the wood has swelled, making them watertight; this usually requires about twenty-four hours. Vintage whiskey barrels, usually made from white oak, can also be used for water gardens, and these barrels are self-sealing. When using whiskey barrels, scrub and rinse the interior well to remove any acids or alcohol before adding water and plants.

Other types of garden barrels can be made watertight using either of two methods. For a water garden that can be assembled in an afternoon, line the barrel with plastic, securing it with staples. Or, for less visible waterproofing, seal the seams of the barrel using a marine-grade sealant or adhesive. Since the sealant requires time to cure between applications, this method requires several days before the water and plants can be added.

For a larger water garden, use a vinyl tub and construct a simple surround for the tub using dimensional cedar lumber. Large, all-purpose tubs are usually available at building supply stores, farm supply stores, and pet supply stores. Cedar lumber is rough on one side and finished on the other; either side may be used for the outer side of the surround, depending on the desired look.

Many nurseries stock a large variety of aquatic plants. Pond plants are also available from mail-order sources. Aquatic plants include those that grow in containers of potted soil submerged below the surface of the water, and floating plants, whose roots dangle in the water. The chart below lists several commonly available aquatic plants. Many traditional potted plants, such as pepper plants, tomatoes, and flowering plants, can be placed in water gardens if the pot is only partially submerged. Select plants in a variety of textures and heights for a pleasing arrangement. In general, do not cover more than three-fourths of the water surface with plants.

Most aquatic plants require full sunlight to develop. Since the sunlight also increases algae growth, you may need to replace the water periodically with fresh water. Floating pond plants, which block the sunlight from the water, will help reduce algae growth.

TYPES OF AQUATIC PLANTS

CONTAINER PLANTS		FLOATING PLANTS
Arrowhead	lizard tail	Water hyacinth
	umbrella palm	
canna		water lettuce
	variegated	
cattail	sweet flag	parrot feather.
dwarf papyrus	water iris	
spike rush	water lilies.	

HOW TO SEAL A WOODEN BARREL USING SEALANT

MATERIALS

- Wooden garden barrel.
- Marine-grade sealant or adhesive.
- Wood shim or old spatula, for spreading sealant.
- 4d finish nails.

1 Tap inside bottom of the barrel, using a hammer, to make sure the base is snug against sides. Using finish nails, nail through the base at an angle into the sides of the barrel, taking care that the nails do not protrude to the outside. Barrel must be thoroughly dry before sealant is applied.

2 Apply sealant liberally around the inside bottom perimeter of barrel, on side seams, and in the center drainage hole, if necessary; spread sealant smooth, using shim or spatula. Apply sealant where nails of the barrel hoop protrude to the inside. Allow sealant to cure, following the manufacturer's directions; then recoat. Allow to cure.

HOW TO LINE A WOODEN BARREL USING PLASTIC

MATERIALS

- Wooden garden barrel.
- Heavy-duty plastic sheeting.
- Staple gun and 5/16" (7.5 mm) staples.
- Utility knife.

1 Cut two sheets of plastic to fit inside barrel with edges extending beyond barrel top; place in barrel. Using hose, partially fill barrel with water and smooth plastic against bottom; fill barrel to depth of about 9" (23 cm). Fold pleats in plastic so it lies smooth against barrel.

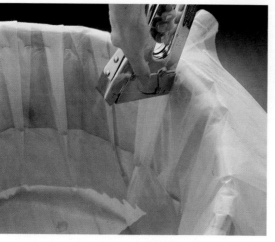

2 Staple plastic to sides of barrel, about 1" (2.5 cm) from upper edge. Position one staple on each side of barrel; then staple about 1" (2.5 cm) apart, folding any additional pleats for a smooth fit.

3 Trim the plastic about ¼" (6 mm) above staples, using utility knife.

HOW TO MAKE A WOOD SURROUND
FOR A TUB-STYLE WATER GARDEN

MATERIALS

- Large vinyl tub.
- 1 × 12 or 1 × 10 cedar board, grade S3S; width of board should be at least equal to depth of tub.
- 1 × 2 cedar board, grade S3S, for upper casing.
- #6 × 2" (5 cm) galvanized deck screws.
- Circular saw or jigsaw; drill; #6 combination drill and countersink bit.

CUTTING DIRECTIONS

Cut, from 1 × 12 or 1 × 10, two boards for the sides of the box, with each board equal to the outer width of the tub plus ½" (1.3 cm). Cut two boards for the front and back pieces, with each board equal to the outer length of the tub plus ½" (1.3 cm) plus twice the thickness of the wood. Lightly sand edges of wood at ends as necessary.

1 Align front piece to one side piece as shown. Drilling through front piece into side piece, predrill holes for screws, using combination drill and countersink bit; countersink the hole up to point indicated by white line (arrow). Secure pieces with screws. Repeat for remaining side piece; then secure back piece.

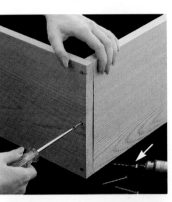

2 Measure outside width of box; from 1 × 2 board, cut two pieces this measurement less 2" (5 cm) for side casing pieces. Center casing on upper edge of surround side piece, with casing extending ¼" (6 mm) beyond inside edge; predrill, and secure with screws. Repeat at opposite side.

3 Measure length of box, measuring from outside edges of casing pieces. From 1 × 2 board, cut two pieces to this measurement for front and back casing pieces. Position casing on upper edge of surround front piece, flush with the side moldings; predrill, and secure with screws.

4 Elevate the tub, if necessary, to within about ½" (1.3 cm) of the surround height; support tub with bricks or pieces of landscape lumber. Place surround around tub.

TIP FOR WATER GARDENING

Place small stones or pea gravel on top of heavy garden soil to prevent it from washing out of the container. Use inverted terra-cotta pots or bricks to adjust the height of container pond plants for the recommended water depth.

GARDEN STONES

Personalize your yard or garden with original stepping stones. Create stones to document special family events, such as birthdays or visits from family members. Make simple imprints in the garden stones, or decorate them with embedded gems or shells.

Made using mortar mix, garden stones are very inexpensive. Mortar mix is available at hardware stores and home center stores, and one bag will make many garden stones. Plastic plant liners and cardboard boxes are used as molds for making the stones.

Because the garden stones do not contain any gravel and are not reinforced, they are somewhat susceptible to breakage. To help prevent breaking, set the stone on a sand base, 1" to 2" (2.5 to 5 cm) in depth.

When making garden stones, work in a well-ventilated area and avoid inhaling dust from the mortar mix. You may want to wear a dust mask and eye protection. Wash thoroughly with water after handling the mortar mixture.

MATERIALS

- Mortar mix.
- Bucket, for mixing mortar.
- Wooden paddle, such as piece of pine lath.
- Metal spatula.
- Sturdy, flat cardboard box, such as a pizza take-out box, for mold of square garden stone.
- Round plastic plant liner, for mold of round garden stone.

HOW TO MAKE A GARDEN STONE

1 **Round stone.** Pour mortar mix into bucket; create a well in center of mix. Add water, and stir until mixture is the consistency of a thick paste; add more water as necessary, small amounts at a time. Mixture should be difficult to stir and not soupy.

2 Place round plastic plant liner on several layers of newspaper. Fill the mold with mortar mix. Using a wooden paddle, smooth the mortar level with the upper edge of the mold; repeat as necessary, adding mortar to any low areas.

3 Smooth surface of the mortar, if desired, using a metal spatula. Allow the mortar to cure for up to 5 minutes.

4 Embed items, such as marbles, beads, tiles, or shells, if desired.

Square stone. Cut lid from cardboard box, and insert it inside the box bottom. Apply packing tape to inside lower edges and inside corners, to seal them. Make garden stone, following steps 1 to 5, above.

5 Allow to dry 5 to 10 minutes. Draw designs, using the point of a pencil or a plastic knife, or make imprints as desired. Allow the mortar to cure for about 3 days. Remove stone from the mold.

BIRDHOUSES

Make a decorative birdhouse for the backyard, and enjoy the activity of nesting birds. This birdhouse is designed to be functional and can be finished for a variety of decorative looks.

The birdhouse is constructed with a floor about 4" (10 cm) square and a height of 8" (20.5 cm). This size is suitable for attracting many species of cavity-nesting birds, as listed in the chart opposite. The recommended diameter of the entrance hole and the height for mounting the birdhouse vary with the species of bird you are trying to attract.

To provide the necessary insulation, use lumber that measures ¾" (2 cm) thick. To allow for cleaning, one side of the house pivots open. This also allows you to monitor the nesting or to remove nests if less desirable birds, such as sparrows, are occupying the birdhouse.

The house is easily made, using 1 × 6 lumber. The actual dimensions of these boards is ¾" × 5½" (2 × 14 cm); however, the measurements may vary slightly. In order for the pieces of the house to fit together accurately, select a board that does measure 5½" (14 cm) in width. For a birdhouse that will withstand the elements for several years, use a long-lasting wood, such as cedar, redwood, or exterior-grade plywood. Pine can also be used; however, it is not as weather-resistant.

When embellishing birdhouses, take a few precautions. Do not apply any paint or preservative to the interior of the house, the inside of the entrance hole, or within ¼" (6 mm) of the entrance hole on the exterior. Avoid painting the house with brightly colored paints, because this may deter birds from using it. If the birdhouse will be hung in direct sunlight, avoid dark colors, because the birdhouse may become too hot.

MATERIALS

- 46" (117 cm) length of 1 × 6 lumber such as cedar, redwood, pine, or exterior-grade plywood.
- 4d galvanized finish nails; drill and 1/16" drill bit.
- Spade bit, sized for desired size of entrance hole, according to chart below.
- Shoulder hook or other latch; screw eyes for hanging birdhouse.
- Handsaw, jigsaw, or circular saw.
- Exterior wood glue.
- 3" (7.5 cm) screws and drill bit, for vertical mounted birdhouse.

CUTTING DIRECTIONS

From 1 × 6 lumber, cut one 4" (10 cm) square for the bottom of house; if using 7/8" (2.2 cm) cedar lumber, cut bottom of house 3¾" × 4" (9.5 × 10 cm). Cut one 5½" × 8¾" (14 × 22.4 cm) piece for the front of the house, two 4" × 5½" (10 × 14 cm) pieces for the sides of the house, and two 5½" × 6½" (14 × 16.3 cm) pieces for the roof of the house. For the back of a hanging birdhouse, cut one 5½" × 8¾" (14 × 22.4 cm) piece; or for the back of a tree-mounted or fence-mounted house, cut one 5½" × 11¾" (14 × 30 cm) piece.

BIRD	DIAMETER OF ENTRANCE HOLE	MOUNTING HEIGHT ABOVE GROUND
CAROLINA WREN	1½" (3.8 cm)	6 ft. to 10 ft. (1.85 to 3.07 m)
CHICKADEE	1⅛" (2.8 cm)	6 ft. to 15 ft. (1.85 to 4.6 m)
DOWNY WOODPECKER	1¼" (3.2 cm)	6 ft. to 20 ft. (1.85 to 6.18 m)
HOUSE WREN & WINTER WREN	1" to 1¼" (2.5 to 3.2 cm)	6 ft. to 10 ft. (1.85 to 3.07 m)
NUTHATCH	1¼" (3.2 cm)	12 ft. to 20 ft. (3.7 to 6.18 m)
TITMOUSE	1¼" (3.2 cm)	6 ft. to 15 ft. (1.85 to 4.6 m)

HOW TO MAKE A HANGING BIRDHOUSE

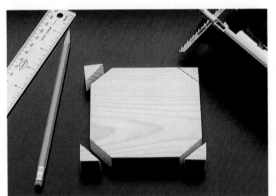

1 Trim the bottom piece diagonally across each corner, ½" (1.3 cm) from corner, to allow for drainage.

2 Mark center of upper edge on front piece. Position a carpenter's square at upper edge. Draw line from center mark to corresponding measurement at the side for pitch of the roof. Repeat for back piece. Cut on marked lines; if using jigsaw, make first cut from peak of roof down to side of house. Then cut opposite side, cutting from side of house toward peak.

3 Mark a line ¾" (2 cm) from the long edge of one roof piece. Cut on marked line so piece measures 4¾" × 6½" (12 × 16.3 cm).

(Continued)

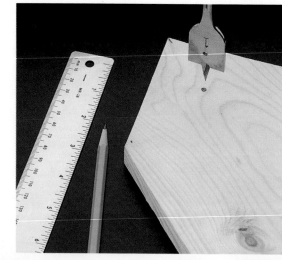

4 Mark a point on front piece, 6¾" (17 cm) from lower edge, centering the mark from side to side. Using spade bit, drill entrance hole, placing the tip of the blade on the marked point. Begin at low speed, gradually increasing speed as bit enters the wood.

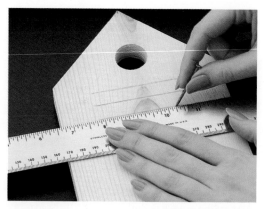

5 Make several deep horizontal scratches below entrance hole on back side of front piece; scratches help young birds grip wood as they climb up to entrance hole.

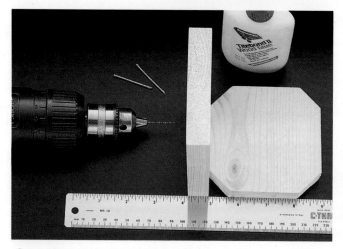

6 Apply wood glue to one side edge of bottom piece; if using ⅞" (2.2 cm) cedar, the 4" (10 cm) edges are the side edges. Align side piece to bottom piece so lower edges are flush. Predrill nail holes through side piece and into bottom, using ¼₆" drill bit; secure with galvanized finish nails.

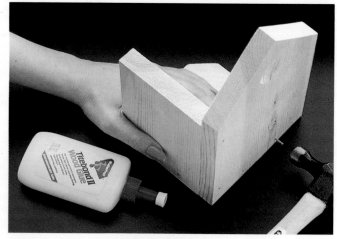

7 Apply wood glue to front edges of side and bottom pieces; align front piece with edges flush. Predrill holes, and secure front piece with nails. Repeat for the back piece.

8 Align, but do not glue, the remaining side piece. Secure front and back pieces to the side piece, inserting one nail through front and one through back; position the nails about ⅝" (1.5 cm) from upper edge. This allows side piece to pivot as shown.

9 Apply glue to the upper edges of front piece and back piece on one side of house; position the shorter roof piece on house, with the back edges flush and with the upper edge of the roof aligned to peak of house.

10 Position the remaining roof piece in place; secure with glue. Predrill holes through both roof pieces; secure with nails.

11 Drill hole for shoulder hook or other latch in side of house front as shown; position the hole about 1" (2.5 cm) from the lower edge of board. Insert the shoulder hook to desired depth and pivot to secure the board or secure the latch.

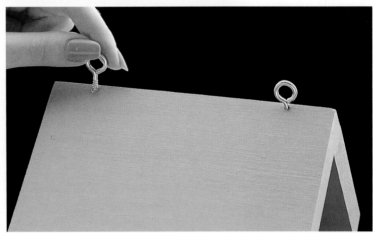

12 Sand edges of birdhouse as necessary. Paint or stain as desired.

13 Attach screw eyes through roof near peak, for hanging birdhouse.

HOW TO MAKE A BIRDHOUSE THAT MOUNTS VERTICALLY

1 Mark a line 3" (7.5 cm) from one short edge of back piece; this is for aligning lower edge of bottom piece. Predrill three holes as shown for mounting birdhouse. Trim back piece diagonally across lower corners, if desired, about 1" (2.5 cm) from corners.

2 Nail two narrow wood strips to back of birdhouse as shown; this allows a space between the house and the surface it is mounted to, preventing any water from collecting and soaking through the back piece. Continue as in steps 1 to 12, pages 43 to 45. Mount to fence post or tree, using screws inserted into drilled holes.

IDEAS FOR DECORATING BIRDHOUSES

Copper roof (right) develops a natural patina over the seasons. The copper sheets are wrapped around the wood roof pieces and nailed in place with copper weatherstrip nails. The birdhouse is painted in a blue-and-white checkerboard pattern.

Miniature doors and windows (left), sold as half-scale miniatures at dollhouse stores, embellish this house. The roof is shingled with dollhouse shakes.

Log-cabin style is created by nailing twigs to the exterior of this redwood birdhouse, and a chimney has been added. A large pinecone, painted green, is used as a pine tree.

Whimsical paint design *is used to personalize a pine birdhouse.*

DECORATIVE BIRD FEEDERS

Log feeder, hung from a tree with twine, has drilled holes packed with suet to feed wintering birds. Dried naturals, secured with wire, embellish the feeder. Clamp log and drill the holes as on page 63, step 2.

Basket becomes a bird feeder when filled with cracked corn and sunflower seeds. Add an edible embellishment, such as miniature Indian corn.

Decorate the backyard while feeding the birds with simple, innovative bird feeders. Although many styles of utilitarian bird feeders can be purchased, these charming feeders are as readily visited by birds and are easy to create. When you are introducing a new feeder, it may take several days or even a few weeks before the birds begin visiting it.

Wooden cutouts (above), covered with birdseed, add a decorative accent to the backyard. Cover the wood with a mixture of peanut butter and honey, and press the birdseed into place. The cutout can be recoated and used many times.

Seed-covered pinecone (above, right) is trimmed with a colorful ribbon. Form a hanger from wire by wrapping it around the top layer of the pinecone. Then spread peanut butter on the cone, roll it in birdseed, and add a pretty ribbon bow.

Straw wreath (right) is embellished with miniature dried sunflowers and artificial berries. A dried sunflower head, glued to the center of the wreath, provides a banquet of seeds.

THE YARD & GARDEN

49

Banners, hung from a flagpole, can add a splash of color to a landscaped area. Or mounted on the side of the house, they become cheerful accents around the exterior. They add a festive touch to celebrations such as birthdays or cookouts and serve as easy-to-spot markers for guests.

Select simple appliqué designs like those shown here. Books, such as coloring books and copyright-free illustration books, offer a wide selection of appliqué ideas that can be enlarged using a photocopy machine. Letter and numeral stencils are available in a variety of sizes and styles at office supply stores. To help you visualize how the appliqués will look on the banner, you may want to cut the designs you plan to use from colored paper or fabric scraps and place them on a sheet of paper the size of the banner.

The banners are constructed using a reversible appliqué technique, so the design of the banner is visible from both sides. When using letters or numerals for the appliqués, hang the banner for one-sided viewing. If the appliqué design extends to the edge of the banner, such as the stem of a flower that extends to the lower edge, the technique for sewing the banner varies slightly, as on page 54.

For a banner that hangs well and can withstand several seasons of outdoor use, select a heavyweight nylon fabric, such as 200-denier nylon, available in several colors. This heavier fabric is especially easy to handle when applying appliqués using the reversible technique.

Banners can be made in any size. If you will be displaying the banner on a wall, measure the space to determine an attractive size. A popular size for banners displayed on flagpoles is 28" × 40" (71 × 102 cm).

If you will be hanging the banner from a flagpole, select a pole that has a screw or clip at the end of the staff. This allows you to fasten a small tab on the banner to the pole, which prevents the banner from shifting downward. Some flagpoles are also designed to allow the banner to spin freely, preventing it from wrapping around the pole.

Banners *add color to the exterior of a home or to a yard. Hang the banner from a pole set (right) or from a flagpole (opposite).*

MATERIALS

- Heavyweight nylon fabric, 200-denier.
- Monofilament nylon thread; machine embroidery thread.
- Water-soluble stabilizer.
- Flagpole and mounting bracket for flagpole, or wood pole set.
- ¼" (6 mm) grosgrain ribbon, for streamers, optional.
- Appliqué scissors.

1 **Designs contained within edges of banner.** Cut the banner from the background fabric, adding 2" (5 cm) to the desired finished width and 5" (12.5 cm) to the desired finished length; this allows for hems and upper casing. Cut appliqués in desired shapes and colors.

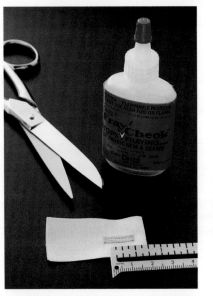

2 Cut one 1" × 4" (2.5 × 10 cm) rectangle for tab from background fabric, if banner will be hung from garden post (page 61) or flagpole; apply liquid fray preventer to raw edges. Fold fabric in half crosswise; stitch ½" (1.3 cm) buttonhole about ¼" (6 mm) from folded edge as shown. Set aside.

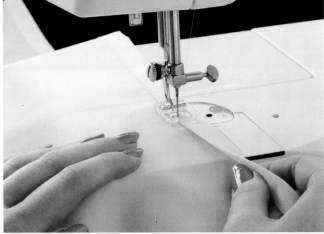

3 Press under ½" (1.3 cm) twice on one long edge of the banner. Straight-stitch close to the first fold, using monofilament thread. Repeat to hem opposite long edge.

4 Press under ½" (1.3 cm) on the upper edge of the banner; then press under 3" (7.5 cm), for casing. For banner with tab, center tab on the foldline of casing, on wrong side of fabric, with folded edge of tab about ⅛" (3 mm) from hemmed edge. Stitch in place as shown.

5 Fold casing in place; pin. Stitch close to first fold; then stitch ¼" (6 mm) above first row of stitching.

6 Press under ½" (1.3 cm) at the lower edge of the banner; then press under 1" (2.5 cm). Pin in place. Stitch close to both folded edges; then stitch another row, centered between previous stitching.

7 Position the appliqué pieces on the banner, and pin in place. For a layered design, pin the first layer only and mark the placement of foreground layers, using water-soluble marking pen or chalk.

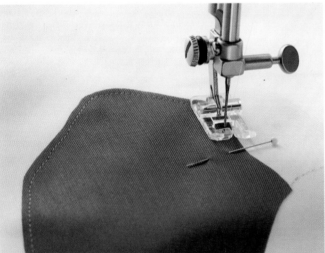

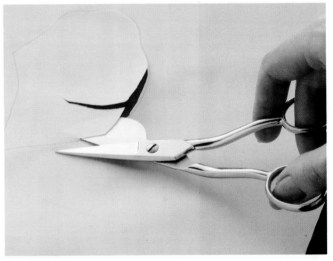

8 Straight-stitch around the appliqué piece, about ⅛" (3 mm) from raw edges, using monofilament thread.

9 Separate the fabric layers, working from back side of banner; trim away background fabric, close to stitching.

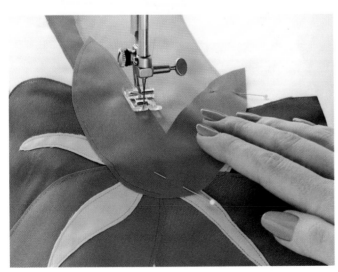

10 Repeat steps 8 and 9 for each background appliqué piece, then for any foreground appliqué pieces.

11 Cut water-soluble stabilizer about 2" (5 cm) larger than the area to be appliquéd. With back side of the banner facing up, position the stabilizer over the appliqué area; pin in place.

(Continued)

12 Set machine for short, wide zigzag stitch; use machine embroidery thread in needle and bobbin. Satin stitch around appliqués, covering raw edges of fabric on front and back of the banner; stitch background appliqués first, then foreground appliqués.

13 Mark any detail lines, such as veins of leaves or flowers, using chalk or water-soluble marking pen. Stitch, tapering zigzag stitching at ends by using narrower stitches.

14 Trim excess stablizer from back side of banner. Mist any remaining stabilizer with water to dissolve it; wipe banner with absorbent paper towel.

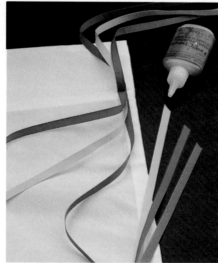

15 Stitch ribbon streamers to upper corner of banner, if desired, stitching over the previous stitching of casing. Apply liquid fray preventer to ends of ribbon to prevent fraying. Hang banner.

1 **Designs extended to edges of banner.** Follow step 1, page 52, cutting appliqué pieces so they extend to raw edge of background fabric. Continue as in steps 2 to 7, except do not stitch hems and casing in place.

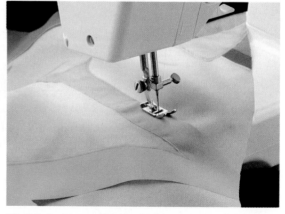

2 Stitch the appliqués as in steps 8 to 10 on page 53, unpinning hems and casing as necessary. Complete banner as in steps 11 to 14. Stitch hems and casing in place.

MORE IDEAS FOR BANNERS

Banner with geometric design is mounted on a wood pole.

Party banner, hung from a flagpole, coordinates with the motif of the party invitation, providing easy identification for arriving guests.

MARK *and* JINNIECE

P I C N I C

WIND SOCKS

Wind socks with brightly colored appliqués are decorative accents for yards or decks. Make a wind sock that can be used year-round, or make several seasonal wind socks.

Sewn from nylon fabric, a wind sock can withstand sunlight, rain, and other weather conditions without fading or deteriorating. Lightweight nylons, such as ripstop, crinkled nylon, and nylon broadcloth, are used because they catch the wind easily. To allow the wind sock to turn freely in the breeze without tangling, it is hung with sturdy nylon cording or fishline attached to a swivel.

A fusible appliqué technique is used for sewing wind socks, making it easy to stitch the appliqués on lightweight nylon without puckering. Draw simple appliqués like those shown on the wind socks above, or enlarge designs from coloring books or seasonal gift-wrapping paper to use as patterns for the appliqués.

The instructions that follow are for a two-color or three-color wind sock with a total of six tails; the finished wind sock is about 37" (94 cm) long and 6" (15 cm) in diameter. You will need 1/2 yd. (0.5 m) of the fabric that will be used for the body of the wind sock; this allows enough fabric for two or three tails from the same color. You will need 1/4 yd. (0.25 m) of the remaining color or colors, allowing enough for appliqués and remaining tails.

MATERIALS

- ½ yd. (0.5 m) fabric, for body of wind sock and tails.
- ¼ yd. (0.25 m) fabric in one or two colors, for appliqués and tails.
- Paper-backed fusible web.
- 19" (48.5 cm) length of heavyweight covered wire.
- Vinyl, waterproof tape.
- 1 yd. (0.95 m) nylon cording or monofilament nylon fishline, for hanging wind sock.
- Wind sock swivel or #5 or #6 ball-bearing swivel for fishing, to be used as hanger.

CUTTING DIRECTIONS

Cut one rectangle, 16½" long × 18½" wide (41.8 × 47.3 cm), from the ½ yd. (0.5 m) piece of fabric, for the body of the wind sock. Cut a total of six tails, 3¼" × 22" (8.2 × 56 cm) each, on the crosswise grain, cutting two or three tails from each color of fabric as desired.

As on page 58, steps 1 and 2, cut the appliqués in the desired shapes and colors, using the remaining fabric.

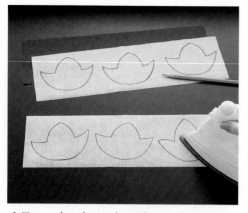

1 Trace the desired appliqué shapes onto paper side of fusible web; for asymmetrical designs, trace the mirror image. Apply fusible web to wrong side of fabric, following the manufacturer's instructions.

2 Cut the appliqué pieces, following marked lines on the fusible web; remove the paper backing.

3 Arrange appliqué pieces on body of wind sock, allowing for ¼" (6 mm) seams at side and lower edges and 1" (2.5 cm) casing at top. Fuse the appliqués in place.

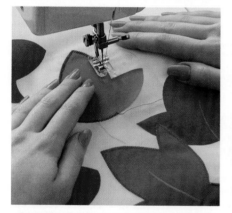

4 Mark any lines for design details. Stitch around appliqués and along the marked lines, using short zigzag stitches of medium width.

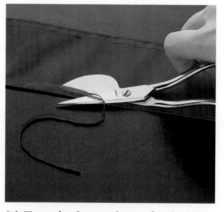

5 Turn the long edges of tails ¼" (6 mm) to wrong side; stitch close to fold. Trim the excess fabric close to the stitching.

6 Turn long edges to wrong side again, enclosing raw edge. Stitch over previous stitches.

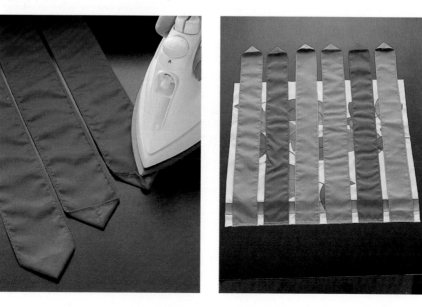

7 Fold lower end of the tail in half, right sides together. Stitch ¼" (6 mm) seam across end. Press seam open. Turn end of the tail right side out, to form a point; press. Stitch and turn the remaining tail ends.

8 Pin the tails evenly along lower edge of the wind sock body, with right sides together and raw edges even; leave ¼" (6 mm) seam allowance on the sides of the body. Stitch ¼" (6 mm) seam along lower edge; finish seam, using zigzag or overlock stitch.

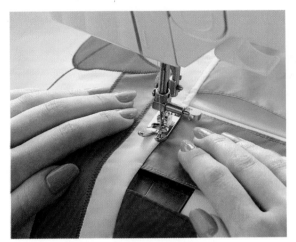

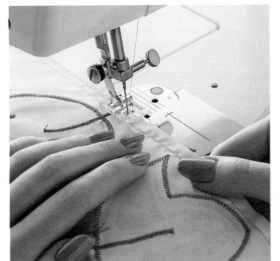

9 Turn seam toward wind sock body, with tails extending down. Topstitch seam in place.

10 Fold wind sock body in half, matching raw edges at the side; stitch ¼" (6 mm) seam. Finish the seam using zigzag or overlock stitch. Turn wind sock right side out.

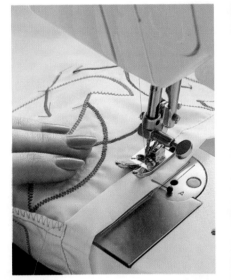

11 Press under ¼" (6 mm) on upper edge of wind sock. Then press under ¾" (2 cm); pin in place, to form a casing. Stitch close to the first fold; leave 2" (5 cm) opening for inserting wire.

12 Insert 19" (48.5 cm) length of covered wire into casing. Wrap overlapped ends of wire together with waterproof tape to secure. Stitch opening in the casing closed.

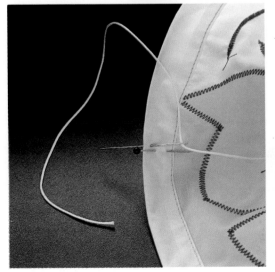

13 Divide the top of wind sock into thirds; mark. At each mark, take a single stitch through the casing, just below the wire, using large-eyed needle and 12" (30.5 cm) length of nylon cording or fishline.

14 Tie end of nylon cording or fishline securely to the wind sock as shown.

15 Hold the ends of the cords together, keeping lengths equal. Thread ends through the eye of the ball-bearing swivel; tie securely. Hang wind sock.

GARDEN POSTS

Add interest to a front entrance or backyard with a garden post. This versatile post can be used to mount a birdhouse or hanging plants, or to hang a banner or wind sock. A finial can be used to embellish the top of the post as shown opposite.

When shopping for the post, be sure to select one that is straight, checking the lumber for a straight vertical grain. Lumber with a straight grain is less likely to warp over time.

Install the garden post by inserting it into a larger pipe that has been set into the ground in cement. This allows for removal of the post if you are mowing the lawn or if you choose to use the post seasonally. You can also replace the post easily should it become damaged over time. Or make various posts for different times of the year, perhaps mounting a birdhouse during nesting season and hanging a banner at Christmas.

When hanging plants from the garden post, reduce the weight of the baskets by using a soilless potting mixture. This lightweight medium has good drainage and will reduce the amount of weight on the post.

Birdhouse, *mounted to the top of a garden post, is decorated with painted vines and flowers that trail down the post. Construct the birdhouse as on pages 43 to 45.*

MATERIALS

GENERAL SUPPLIES

- 8-ft. (2.48 m) length of 2 × 2 S4S cedar post.

- Finial to fit diameter of 2" (5 cm) wood post; finial intended for use with wooden drapery pole may be used.

- Exterior primer for wood; exterior paint.

- Premixed concrete.

- Coarse gravel, such as ¾ gravel or pea stone.

- 16" (40.5 cm) length of UV-resistant PVC plastic pipe with 2" (5 cm) inside diameter.

- Jigsaw.

FOR POST WITH BIRDHOUSE

- Scrap pieces of 1 × lumber, ¾" (2 cm) thick.

- Drill and ½" drill bit.

FOR POST WITH BANNER

- ¾" (2 cm) hardwood dowel, for banner pole.

- 1" (2.5 cm) ball knob and knob hanger bolt; or any finial designed for use with a ¾" (2 cm) pole may be used.

- Drill and ¾" (2 cm) spade bit.

- 1" (2.5 cm) galvanized finish nail; short brass wood screw.

FOR POST WITH WIND SOCK

- ¾" (2 cm) hardwood dowel, for wind sock pole.

- 1" (2.5 cm) ball knob and knob hanger bolt; or any finial designed for use with a ¾" (2 cm) pole may be used.

- Drill and ¾" (2 cm) spade bit.

- 1" (2.5 cm) galvanized finish nail; brass screw eye.

Garden posts can be used for displaying banners or wind socks (above) or hanging baskets (below).

HOW TO MAKE A GARDEN POST FOR A BIRDHOUSE

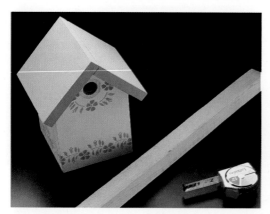

1 Make the birdhouse, following instructions for hanging birdhouse on pages 43 to 45, steps 1 to 12. Cut the post 16" (40.5 cm) longer than desired height of post.

2 Cut platform from 7½" (19.3 cm) square of scrap lumber. Cut a 4" (10 cm) square piece of paper; center paper on platform, and mark corners, using pencil. Using ⅜" or ½" drill bit, drill a hole just inside marked corners, to align with drainage holes in bottom of the birdhouse.

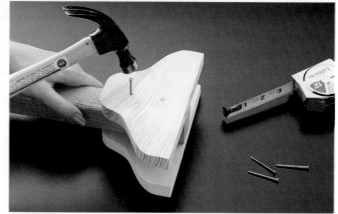

3 Make paper pattern for brackets by folding a 4" × 7" (10 × 18 cm) piece of paper in half crosswise; mark the curved lower edge as desired. Cut on marked line; unfold the paper. Trace around bracket pattern on scrap lumber; repeat to mark second bracket on lumber. Cut brackets.

4 Center one bracket on the post, aligning upper edges. Secure with nails positioned ¾" (2 cm) and 2¼" (6 cm) from upper edge. Secure remaining bracket on opposite side of post, offsetting nails ½" (1.3 cm) lower than for first bracket.

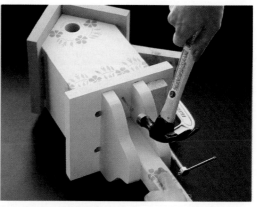

5 Center platform on post. Drilling from the top of platform into bracket, predrill the holes for nails. Secure the platform with nails.

6 Apply primer to post, brackets, and platform. Apply second coat of primer to the ends and lower 20" (51 cm) of the post. Paint as desired.

7 Center birdhouse on platform; clamp in place. Mark the location for two nails on platform, taking care that nails will penetrate the center bottom piece of birdhouse. Predrill from bottom of platform into the birdhouse; secure with nails. Set post (page 64).

HOW TO MAKE A GARDEN POST FOR A BANNER

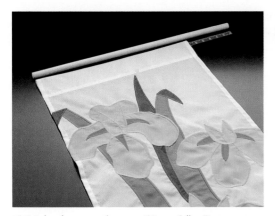

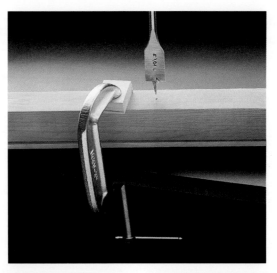

1 Make banner (pages 50 to 54). Cut post 16" (40.5 cm) longer than desired height of post. Cut dowel for banner pole 6" (15 cm) longer than width of banner.

2 Mark post for placement of pole, centering the marking. Clamp post to the work surface, placing a scrap of lumber under area to be drilled; also use scraps of lumber to protect upper surface of post from clamps. Drill hole through post at the marking, using 3/4" (2 cm) spade bit.

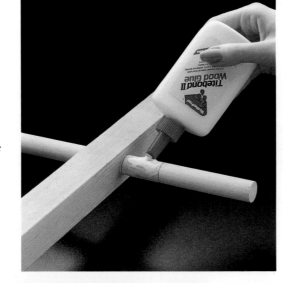

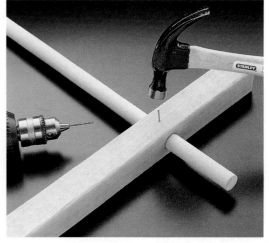

3 Mark the dowel 3½" and 5" (9 and 12.5 cm) from end. Insert dowel through hole in post up to 5" (12.5 cm) marking; apply wood glue around the dowel, to area between markings. Slide dowel into post up to 3½" (9 cm) marking.

4 Predrill hole through post and into dowel, using 1/16" drill bit; secure the dowel, using finish nail.

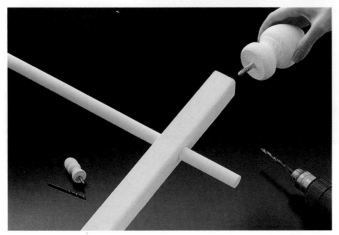

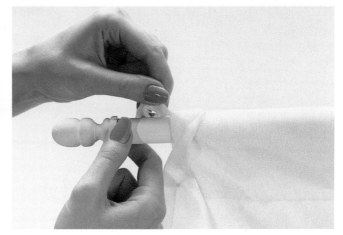

5 Paint post, pole, and finials as in step 6, opposite. Secure finial to top of the post, predrilling for screw hole; size of the drill bit should be equal to diameter of core of screw. Predrill hole in the end of dowel for finial.

6 Set post (page 64). Hang banner on pole; secure finial. Secure banner to dowel by inserting small wood screw at top of pole, aligning screw with tab of banner. Position buttonhole of tab over screw head.

HOW TO MAKE A GARDEN POST FOR A WIND SOCK

1 Make wind sock (pages 56 to 59). Cut the post 16" (40.5 cm) longer than desired height of the post. Cut the dowel for wind sock pole 20" (51 cm) long.

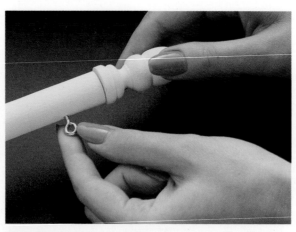

2 Follow steps 2 to 5 for garden post for banner (page 63). Insert screw eye on underside of the wind sock pole, 1" (2.5 cm) from end.

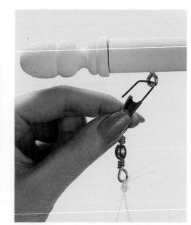

3 Set post (below). Secure swivel of wind sock to the screw eye.

HOW TO MAKE A GARDEN POST FOR HANGING PLANTS

1 Cut post 16" (40.5 cm) longer than desired height of post. Paint post and finials as in step 6 (page 62). Secure finial to top of post, predrilling for screw hole; size of drill bit should be equal to diameter of core of the screw.

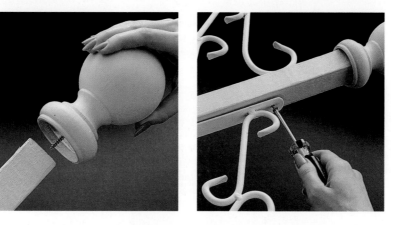

2 Secure one bracket each to two opposite sides of post. Offset vertically to prevent the post from warping due to uneven weight distribution. Set post (below). Hang planters of equal size and weight.

HOW TO SET A GARDEN POST

1 Dig a post hole about 18" (46 cm) deep. Pour a 2" (5 cm) layer of gravel into the hole, to allow water to drain away from post.

2 Place PVC pipe into hole; top of pipe should be about ½" (1.3 cm) above the ground. Insert post into the pipe. Have an assistant hold the post straight, using levels placed on two adjacent sides of post. Fill the hole with soil to within about 6" (15 cm) from ground level.

3 Mix cement, following the manufacturer's directions; pour into hole. Shape concrete around the top of pipe to form a slightly rounded crown. Carefully remove garden post. Allow the concrete to cure for 48 hours; reinsert post.

MORE IDEAS FOR GARDEN POSTS

Signpost *(right) is created by hanging an address signboard on a garden post.*

Bird feeder *(below) is mounted on a garden post. The feeder is constructed as a simple framework with a screen for the bottom to allow for drainage.*

356
SAGE ST.

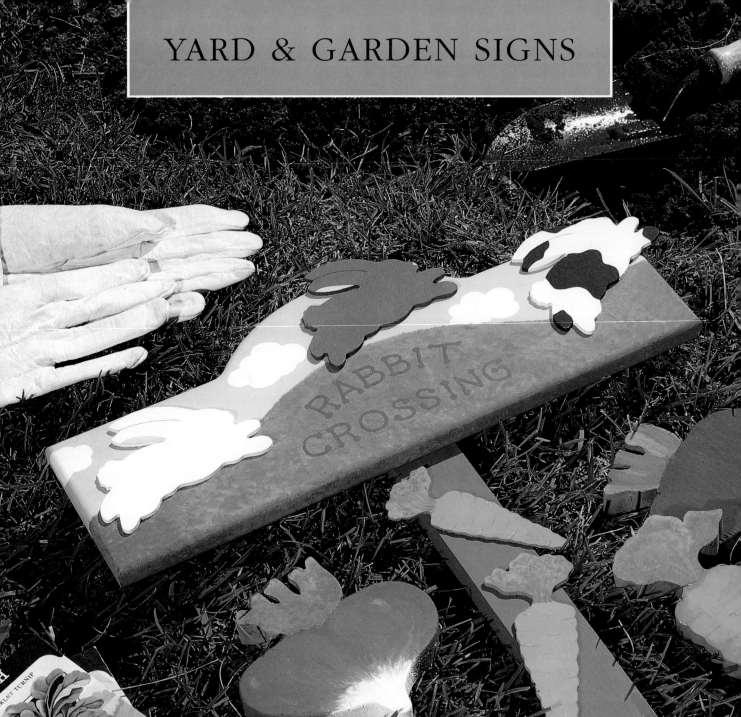

Painted signs can add a splash of color and a touch of whimsy to the yard or garden. You can use the preassembled, unfinished wooden signs that are available in a variety of sizes and styles at craft stores. Purchased wooden cutouts, attached to wooden stakes, also make interesting signs. Or make your own custom signs, using a jigsaw and scraps of lumber.

Embellish the signs with lettering and simple painted designs, using items such as stencils, cookie cutters, or coloring books for inspiration. Small wooden cutouts can also be used as embellishments on larger signs.

Garden markers (opposite) can be used to identify new plantings and add color to the garden.

Party sign (right) welcomes guests and directs them to a backyard party.

TIPS FOR MAKING SIGNS

Use permanent opaque paint pens for lettering, or paint messages on the signs with a fine liner brush. If the signs are painted with acrylic craft paints, spray them with an aerosol clear acrylic sealer for more durability; signs painted with exterior paints do not require a sealer.

Apply wooden cutouts to signs, using exterior wood glue. For best adhesion, glue bare surfaces of wood together.

Make a stake for wooden cutouts by nailing a length of pine parting stop, a ½" (1.3 cm) square dowel, or purchased plant stakes to back of the sign; or secure stakes to the signs with exterior wood glue.

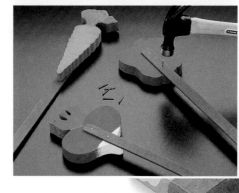

HAMMOCKS

Relax in your backyard or porch in a colorful, decorative hammock. Simple to sew, the hammock is made using decorator fabric for the hammock front and is lined with sturdy canvas. Closet-pole rods and nylon rope support the hammock. The instructions that follow are for a hammock bed that measures about 49" × 77" (125 × 195.5 cm).

Metal rings are secured to each end of the hammock, so the hammock can easily hang on a purchased hammock frame. Or, suspend the hammock between trees by securing additional lengths of rope to the metal rings and tying the hammock to the trees. Although hammocks are often hung from large hooks screwed into the trunks of trees, this technique is not recommended, especially for trees with a trunk diameter less than 12" (30.5 cm), because it exposes the tree to disease.

MATERIALS

- 2¾ yd. (2.55 m) outer fabric, 54" (137 cm) wide.
- 2¾ yd. (2.55 m) heavy-duty canvas, 54" (137 cm) wide, for lining.
- Two 50" (127 cm) lengths of hardwood closet pole, 1¼" (3.2 cm) in diameter.
- Drill and ½" spade bit.
- Exterior primer; exterior paint.
- 40 ft. (12.28 m) of braided nylon rope, ⅜" (1 cm) in diameter; bodkin.
- Two #2 × 2" (5 cm) steel rings.

CUTTING DIRECTIONS

Cut one 53" × 78" (134.5 × 198 cm) rectangle from the outer fabric, trimming the selvages. Cut one 52" × 78" (132 × 198 cm) rectangle from the canvas lining, trimming the selvages. For the pole sleeves, cut two 8" × 45" (20.5 × 115 cm) rectangles each from the outer fabric and the lining.

HOW TO MAKE A HAMMOCK

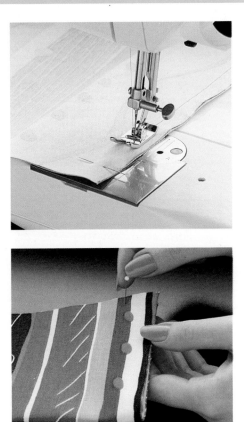

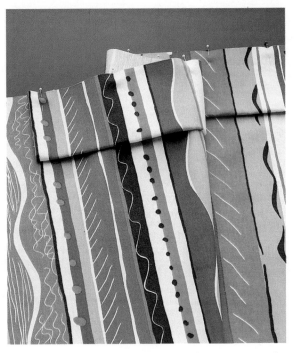

1 Pin outer fabric and lining for one pole sleeve, right sides together, matching raw edges. Stitch ½" (1.3 cm) seams at short ends. Repeat for remaining pole sleeve.

2 Press the seam allowances open. Turn right side out; press. Fold one pole sleeve in half lengthwise, wrong sides together; pin along raw edges. Repeat for remaining pole sleeve.

3 Pin-mark center of each pole sleeve; pin-mark center of hammock outer fabric at the upper and lower edges. Pin one sleeve to right side of hammock outer fabric at each end, matching pin marks and raw edges; outer fabric extends beyond sleeves at sides. Machine-baste a scant ½" (1.3 cm) from raw edges.

(Continued)

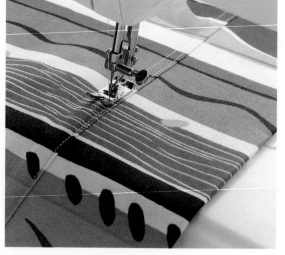

4 Pin hammock lining and outer fabric, right sides together, along upper and lower edges; center lining so outer fabric extends ½" (1.3 cm) beyond lining at the sides. Stitch ½" (1.3 cm) seams.

5 Turn hammock right side out; press. Topstitch ⅛" and ⅜" (3 mm and 1 cm) from seam.

6 Place the hammock on a smooth, flat surface, lining side up. Pin the fabric and the lining together at sides, about 5" (12.5 cm) from raw edges of outer fabric.

7 Press up ½" (1.3 cm) along the edge of outer fabric, encasing the raw edges of the lining. Then press outer fabric and lining up 1½" (3.8 cm); pin.

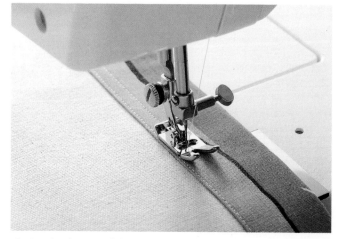

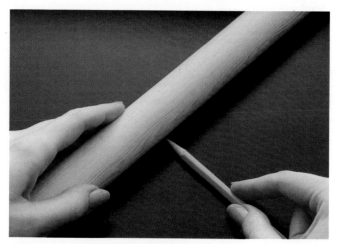

8 Stitch close to folded edge to make casing; stitch again ¼" (6 mm) from first row of stitching.

9 Hold pole firmly against table; using pencil placed flat on table, draw line on pole.

10 Mark a point on line 1" (2.5 cm) from each end. Clamp pole to work surface, placing a scrap of lumber under the pole at marking. Using a ½" (1.3 cm) spade bit and placing the point of bit at the marking, drill a hole; repeat at the opposite end. Drill holes at the ends of remaining pole.

11 Apply primer to poles, applying two coats at the ends. Paint the poles as desired.

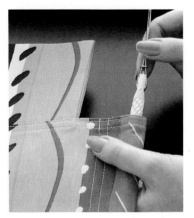

12 Cut the rope in half; wrap the ends with masking tape to prevent raveling. Using a bodkin, thread the rope through the side casing, with ends extending evenly. Repeat to thread the rope through opposite casing.

13 Spread the hammock on smooth, flat surface. Insert a pole into each rod sleeve. Tie an overhand knot about 1½" (3.8 cm) beyond the end of casing. Thread rope through the hole in pole, and push pole firmly against the knot. Tie a second overhand knot to secure the dowel. Repeat at each corner of hammock, making sure there is no slack in the rope.

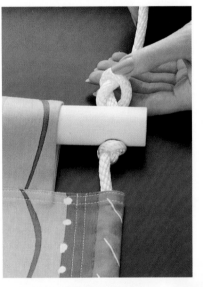

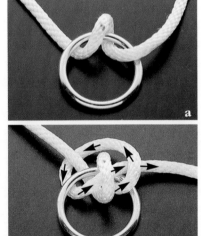

14 Secure ropes to metal rings for hanging the hammock; the length of ropes depends on distance between hammock frame or trees. Mark dots on ropes at desired length. Secure one rope at one end of the hammock to a ring, using fisherman's bend knot as shown as in photos **a** and **b.**

15 Secure free end of rope with two half hitches as shown. Secure remaining rope at this end of hammock; then secure ropes to ring at opposite end of hammock.

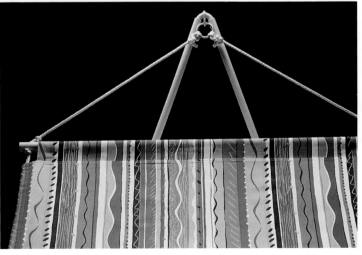

16 Hang the hammock on hammock frame or secure to trees, using additional length of rope.

The Porch & Patio

TABLECLOTHS FOR UMBRELLA-STYLE TABLES

Round and oval tables with a center umbrella are popular tables for patios and decks. Add a splash of color to these tables by making custom-size tablecloths. For ease in use, the tablecloth is constructed with a side opening to avoid having to remove the umbrella when positioning the tablecloth. To prevent the wind from blowing the tablecloth up onto the table, drapery weights are stitched along the lower edge of the tablecloth.

For tablecloths with body, select firmly woven, mediumweight fabrics, such as poplin or denim. It is often necessary to seam two or more lengths of fabric together for the desired width. If the fabric width being added to the full fabric width is 10" (25.5 cm) or narrower, stitch the additional fabric width to one side of the full fabric width; the seam falls within the drop length of the tablecloth and is not noticeable. If the additional width needed is more than 10" (25.5 cm), use the full fabric width in the center and stitch narrower side panels to both sides; this positions the seams evenly on each side of the table.

When determining yardage, allow for the placket strips and facing. If you are piecing two lengths of fabric for the necessary width, you will usually have sufficient excess fabric to cut these pieces.

MATERIALS

- Fabric; scrap of nonwoven interfacing.
- Hook and loop tape, ¾" (2 cm) wide.
- Plastic-covered drapery weights.

CUTTING DIRECTIONS

For a round table, measure the diameter of the table; add 20" (51 cm) to determine the measurement for the finished tablecloth. This allows for a 10" (25.5 cm) drop length, or overhang. Cut a square of fabric 1" (2.5 cm) larger than this size; piece two fabric widths together, if necessary, and press the seams open.

For an oval table, measure the center length and width of the table; add 20" (51 cm) to each measurement to determine the dimensions for the finished tablecloth; this allows for a 10" (25.5 cm) drop length, or overhang. Cut a rectangle of fabric 1" (2.5 cm) larger than this size; piece two fabric widths together, if necessary, and press the seams open.

HOW TO SEW A TABLECLOTH FOR AN UMBRELLA TABLE

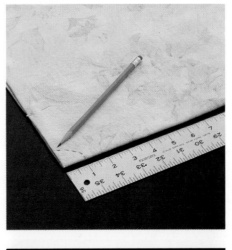

2 Mark an arc, using straight-edge and pencil, measuring 1" (2.5 cm) from the folded center of the fabric.

1 Round tablecloth. Fold square of fabric in half lengthwise, then crosswise. Pin the layers together. Divide measurement for the finished tablecloth by two and add ¼" (6 mm), to determine the radius of cut circle. Mark an arc, measuring from folded center of fabric, a distance equal to radius.

3 Cut on the marked lines through all layers. Cut along one folded edge; this will be the opening of the tablecloth.

(Continued)

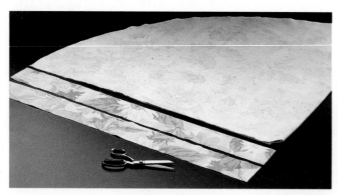

4 Cut two 3" (7.5 cm) strips of fabric for placket opening with the length of each strip equal to the cut length of tablecloth opening plus 1" (2.5 cm).

5 Cut an 8" (20.5 cm) fabric square for facing; fold square in half lengthwise, then crosswise. Mark an arc, measuring 3" (7.5 cm) from folded center of the fabric. Mark a second arc 1" (2.5 cm) from folded center.

6 Cut the fabric on marked lines; cut along one folded edge.

7 Finish the outer curved edge of the facing, using an overlock or zigzag stitch. Pin facing to the tablecloth, with right sides together and raw edges even. Stitch 1/4" (6 mm) seam around center of facing. Clip seam allowances.

8 Press the seam allowances toward facing. Understitch by stitching on right side of the facing, close to seamline. Press the facing to underside of tablecloth.

9 Press under scant 1/2" (1.3 cm) on one long edge of placket. Pin placket to opening edge of tablecloth, with the right sides together and raw edges even; extend the ends of placket 1/2" (1.3 cm) beyond edges of tablecloth. Stitch 1/2" (1.3 cm) seam.

10 Press the seam allowances toward the placket. Fold placket right sides together, with the folded edge of placket extending scant 1/8" (3 mm) beyond seamline; pin. Using a piece of paper folded in quarters, mark an arc 1 1/4" (3.2 cm) from folded center; cut on marked line. Unfold paper pattern to make a circle. Using circle pattern, mark curved seamline on placket. Stitch on marked line; trim seam.

11 Turn placket right side out, with pressed edge of the placket just covering seam on back of tablecloth; pin. Stitch in the ditch on tablecloth top by stitching over the seamline in the well of the seam; catch the placket on the back of the tablecloth in the stitching.

12 Trim ends of placket even with the outside edge of tablecloth. Apply second placket to remaining opening edge, following steps 9 to 11, opposite.

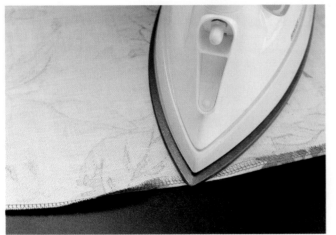

13 Finish raw edge of tablecloth, using an overlock or zigzag stitch. Press fabric ¼" (6 mm) from the edge. Machine-stitch hem in place.

14 Cut hook and loop tape into 1" (2.5 cm) strips. Pin the hook side of tape to overlap, centering tape on the placket; stitch around tape. Pin loop side of tape to placket underlap, directly under hook side of tape; stitch. Repeat to position hook and loop tape at about 6" (15 cm) intervals.

15 Secure drapery weights along the lower edge of the tablecloth at about 24" (61 cm) intervals; reinforce the fabric at stitching line with small piece of firm, non-woven interfacing.

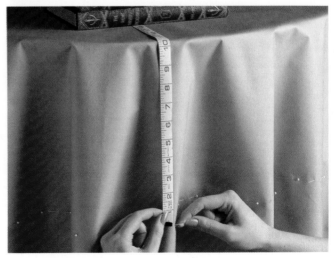

Oval tablecloth. Fold square of fabric in half lengthwise, then crosswise. Pin layers together. Follow steps 2 to 12; in step 3, cut along one of the short folded edges. Place tablecloth on table; weight fabric down. Measure and mark around tablecloth, an amount equal to the desired drop length plus ¼" (6 mm). Cut on marked line. Complete the tablecloth as in steps 13 to 15.

TABLECLOTHS FOR PICNIC TABLES

Tablecloths for rectangular or square picnic tables are quick to make. Grommets, positioned at each corner of the tablecloth, allow the fabric to be laced and cinched at each corner, helping to hold the tablecloth in place. If desired, buttonholes can be substituted for the grommets. This tablecloth style is also useful on card tables, when extra table space is needed for outdoor entertaining.

For durable tablecloths, select firmly woven fabrics, such as poplin or denim. It is often necessary to seam two lengths of fabric together for the desired width. If the panel being added to the full fabric width is 10" (25.5 cm) or narrower, stitch the panel to one side of the full fabric width; the seam falls within the drop length, or overhang, of the tablecloth and will not be noticeable. If the panel is wider than 10" (25.5 cm), use the full fabric width in the center and stitch narrower side panels to both sides; this positions the seams evenly on each side of the table. For a light-weight tablecloth that does not require piecing, use a flat bed sheet.

MATERIALS

- Fabric.
- Size 0 or ¼" (6 mm) grommets; attaching tool.
- 2½ yd. (2.3 m) braided lacing or ribbon.
- Craft wire, for securing ends of lacing, and four conchos, optional.

CUTTING DIRECTIONS

Measure the length and the width of the table. Add 20" (51 cm) to each measurement to determine the dimensions of the finished tablecloth; this allows for a 10" (25.5 cm) drop length, or overhang. Cut a rectangle of fabric 1" (2.5 cm) larger than this size; piece the fabric widths together, if necessary, and press the seams open.

HOW TO SEW A TABLECLOTH FOR A PICNIC TABLE

1 Press under ½" (1.3 cm) on each side of the fabric. Unfold the corner; fold diagonally so pressed folds match. Press diagonal fold; trim corner as shown.

2 Fold under raw edge ¼" (6 mm). Press double-fold hem in place.

3 Stitch hem close to inner fold, pivoting at corners; do not stitch along folds of miter.

4 Place tablecloth on table; pin-mark the grommet placement about 3" (7.5 cm) in from corner of table and 5" (12.5 cm) below the upper edge of table. Repeat at opposite side of corner and remaining corners to mark for eight grommets.

5 Attach grommets securely, following the manufacturer's directions.

6 Reposition tablecloth. Cut braided lacing into four equal lengths; wrap ends with craft wire, or tie knots. Insert lacing through grommets at each corner, and secure concho or tie knot, cinching fabric. If table style allows, lace behind table leg for more secure placement.

TABLECLOTHS
WITH STREAMERS

For a fanciful table setting, make a circular tablecloth with brightly colored streamers. This easy project does not require any sewing. The unfinished edges of the fabrics give a textural effect, and, with repeated washings, the edges curl and fray for even more texture.

The diameter of the tablecloth, not including streamers, is equal to the diameter of the table plus 8" to 10" (20.5 to 25.5 cm), to allow for a 4" to 5" (10 to 12.5 cm) drop length, or overhang. The streamers, cut from 45" (115 cm) fabric, extend almost to the ground.

MATERIALS

- Tightly woven fabric, 45" to 60" (115 to 152.5 cm) wide, for tablecloth; to avoid piecing, select fabric at least 8" (20.5 cm) wider than diameter of table.

- Tightly woven fabrics in several colors, 45" (115 cm) wide, for streamers.

HOW TO MAKE A TABLECLOTH WITH STREAMERS

1 Divide diameter of tablecloth (opposite) by two to determine the radius. Fold tablecloth fabric in half lengthwise, then crosswise, with right sides together. Using a straightedge and pencil, mark an arc on fabric, measuring from the folded center, a distance equal to the radius of the tablecloth. Cut on marked line through all layers. Unfold fabric.

2 Fold up the edge of tablecloth about 1" (2.5 cm). Cut slash from folded edge up to ½" or ¾" (1.3 or 2 cm) from the raw edge, through both layers of folded fabric; when unfolded, slash is about ¾" (2 cm) long. Continue to cut slashes around the tablecloth at about 2" (5 cm) intervals.

3 Trim off selvages of fabric for the streamers. Clip one lengthwise edge of fabric for streamers at 2" (5 cm) intervals, and tear 2" (5 cm) strips across the width of the fabric. Repeat for remaining streamer fabrics.

4 Place tablecloth on patio table, with an even drop length on all sides. Insert streamer into slash of tablecloth, pulling it through about halfway; tie overhand knot. Repeat for remaining streamers, staggering the lengths by pulling them through the slashes to different lengths; distribute colors evenly.

MORE IDEAS FOR TABLE LINENS

Padded placemats *are sewn following the instructions for the chair pads (page 88) for a coordinated look.*

Vinyl placemats with pinked edges *are practical and quick to make. Button the napkins to a patio tablecloth, to prevent them from blowing away. Stitch the buttons to the tablecloth, and stitch a buttonhole in one corner of each napkin.*

CUSHIONS FOR OUTDOOR FURNITURE

For comfort and good looks, make custom-fitted cushions for your outdoor chairs and chaise lounges. Covered with the fabric of your choice, these 3" (7.5 cm) cushions are filled with polyester upholstery batting.

The cushions are sewn with a mock box construction. Stitching lines across the width of the cushions add styling and allow the cushions to conform to the shape of the furniture, bending at the back of the seat and, for chaise lounges, creating a leg rest. Another stitching line across the upper back creates a headrest.

For practical cushions, select water-resistant fabric that is intended for outdoor use, usually from acrylic or polyester. Cotton fabrics may also be used, but they tend to fade in the sunlight. If decorator fabrics that have not been treated for water resistance are used, the cushions should not be left in the rain; when the

water penetrates the fabric and the filling becomes soaked, it is difficult to dry the cushions out.

Outdoor furniture varies widely in style and construction, and includes pieces with frames made from aluminum, wrought iron, steel, and wood. Many have decks of vinyl strapping, wicker, or aluminum mesh. Depending on the furniture style, the cushions may be secured with ties or with the addition of a hooded back piece.

MATERIALS

• Water-repellant fabric intended for outdoor use.

• Polyester upholstery batting.

• Aerosol adhesive intended for use with polyurethane foam.

Ties *may be secured around the frame of many metal and wooden furniture pieces, sometimes inserted through the openwork of a mesh deck or between straps, bars, or slats. For a cushion that is completely reversible, stitch the ties at the side seams.*

Hooded back piece *fits over the back of a chair or chaise lounge. Hooded backs are necessary for furniture pieces that do not have any open areas for ties, such as the fine metal mesh chair shown here.*

HOW TO MAKE A CUSHION WITH ROUNDED CORNERS

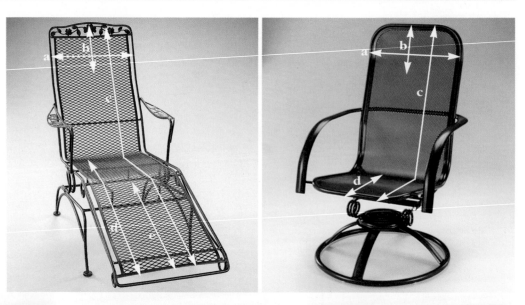

1 Measure width of chair or chaise frame from side to side **(a).** Measure distance from top of frame to desired depth of headrest **(b).** Measure continuous length of chair or chaise lounge frame from top edge of back to front edge of frame **(c).** Measure distance from front edge of frame to back of seat **(d);** if chaise lounge has curved or bent leg rest area, also measure depth of leg rest from front edge of frame to highest point on frame **(e).** Record measurements.

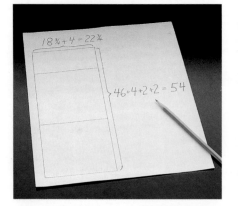

2 Add 4" (10 cm) to length and width, to allow for thickness of cushion and seam allowances. To the length, also add 2" (5 cm) for each stitching line across the cushion. Cut two pieces of fabric to this size.

3 Mark the upper and lower curved corners of frame on paper. Trim paper along the curved lines.

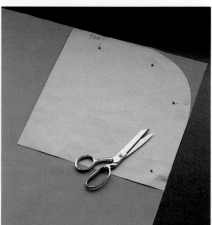

4 Place pattern for curves at corners of fabric, with marked lines tapering to raw edges at upper and side edges; pin in place. Trim fabric along curves.

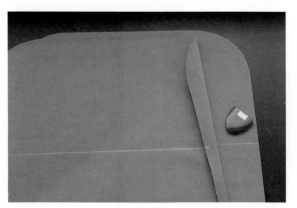

5 Measure from upper edge of fabric a distance equal to the desired depth of headrest plus 3" (7.5 cm). Mark a line on right sides of pieces, across the width, using chalk. Mark ends of line on wrong sides.

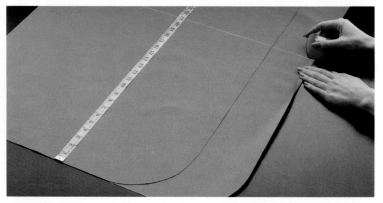

6 **Chair or chaise lounge with a straight leg extension.** Measure from lower edge of fabric a distance equal to the measurement from front of frame to back of seat plus 3" (7.5 cm). Mark a line on right sides of pieces, across the width, using chalk. Mark ends of line on wrong sides of fabric pieces.

6 Chaise lounge with a curved or bent leg rest. Measure from lower edge of fabric a distance equal to depth of leg rest plus 3" (7.5 cm); mark a line on right sides of fabric, across the width, using chalk. Also measure from lower edge of fabric a distance equal to measurement from front of frame to back of seat plus 5" (12.5 cm); mark line on right sides of fabric pieces. Mark ends of both lines on wrong sides of fabric pieces.

7 Cut and attach hood piece, if desired (page 87). Place front and back cushion pieces right sides together; pin, matching marks on the sides.

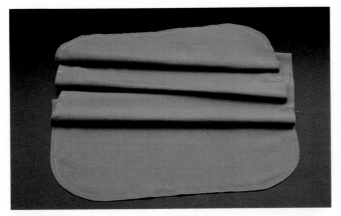

8 Machine-stitch ½" (1.3 cm) from raw edges, starting on one long side, just beyond rounded corner; stitch across end, down opposite long side, across opposite end, and stop just beyond last corner.

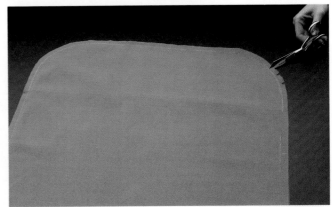

9 Stitch ½" (1.3 cm) from raw edges, on remaining long side, starting and stopping 2" (5 cm) from each marked line; this leaves an opening in each section of cushion. Clip seam allowances of rounded corners.

10 Turn cover right side out through one opening. Make and position ties, if desired (page 87). On sides of cushion, fold 1" (2.5 cm) inverted tucks at stitching lines as shown, and pin in place; enclose ties, if any, in tucks. Pin front and back cushion pieces together along stitching lines.

11 Stitch along the marked stitching lines, stitching tucks in place at sides. If cushion has ties, catch the ties in stitching of tucks.

(Continued)

12 Cut four pieces of polyester upholstery batting for area at top of cushion, cutting pieces 1" (2.5 cm) wider than chair or chaise lounge frame and 1" (2.5 cm) longer than the depth of headrest; round corners. Stack and secure two pieces of batting together, applying aerosol adhesive to both inner sides. Repeat to secure all four layers.

13 Repeat step 12 for section at bottom of cushion, using four pieces of batting 1" (2.5 cm) wider than frame and 1" (2.5 cm) longer than measurement from front of frame to back of seat; if making cushion for chaise lounge with leg rest, use pieces 1" (2.5 cm) longer than depth of leg rest.

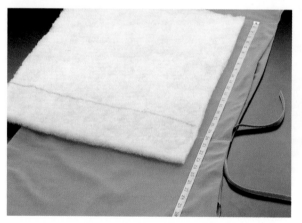

14 Repeat step 12 for middle section or sections of cushion, using pieces of batting cut 1" (2.5 cm) wider than frame, with length of pieces equal to the distance between stitching lines minus 1" (2.5 cm).

15 Fold layered batting for headrest in half crosswise; insert into headrest area through opening, pulling batting all the way to opposite side of cushion. Unfold batting to smooth in place. Adjust position of batting as necessary; fill corners with pieces of batting, if necessary.

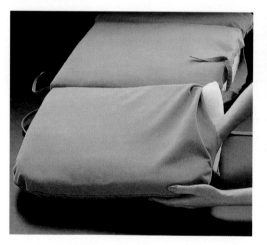

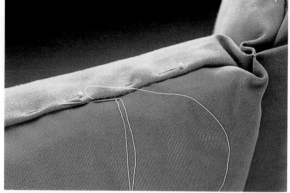

16 Repeat step 15 for the remaining areas of cushion, using corresponding sections of the batting.

17 Pin the openings on side of cushion closed; slipstitch.

HOW TO MAKE A CUSHION WITH SQUARE CORNERS

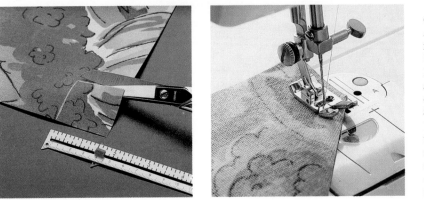

1 Measure chair or chaise lounge frame and cut the fabric as on page 84, steps 1 and 2. At corners, mark a 1½" (3.8 cm) square, using chalk; cut on marked lines.

2 Fold corners, matching the raw edges; stitch a ½" (1.3 cm) seam, 2" (5 cm) long as shown. Complete cushion as on pages 84 to 86, steps 5 to 17; in step 7, fold the corner seam allowances of front and back pieces in opposite directions, to distribute bulk.

HOW TO MAKE & ATTACH A HOODED BACK

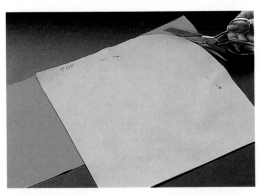

1 Cut fabric for hood piece, 4" (10 cm) wider than the width of chair or chaise lounge frame and 8½" (21.8 cm) long. For cushion with rounded corners, trim upper corners of hood, using paper pattern for upper corners from step 3 on page 84.

2 Press under ½" (1.3 cm) twice on lower edge of hood piece, to the wrong side; stitch to make double-fold hem.

3 Pin hood piece to cushion back piece, right sides up; machine-baste a scant ½" (1.3 cm) from raw edges. Complete cushion as on pages 85 and 86, steps 7 to 17.

HOW TO MAKE & POSITION TIES

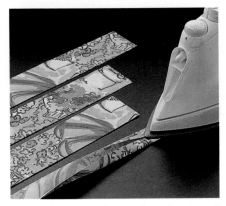
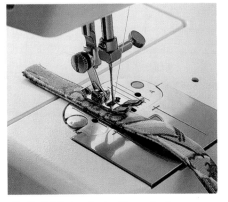
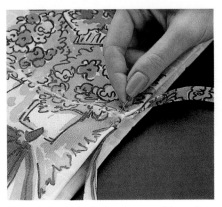

1 Cut four 2" × 24" (5 × 61 cm) strips of fabric, for ties. Press in half lengthwise, wrong sides together; unfold. Fold raw edges to the center; press.

2 Refold ties in half, enclosing raw edges. Edgestitch close to both long edges of ties.

3 Position and pin ties to sides of cushion at marked stitching lines for headrest and back of seat. Complete cushion as on pages 85 and 86, steps 10 to 17.

CHAIR & BENCH PADS

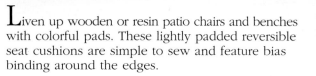

Liven up wooden or resin patio chairs and benches with colorful pads. These lightly padded reversible seat cushions are simple to sew and feature bias binding around the edges.

Make your own bias binding for a customized look, using a bias tape maker as shown on page 91. Or, for quick construction, use purchased bias binding.

MATERIALS

• Decorator fabric.

• ½" (1.3 cm) high-density firm polyurethane foam.

• ½" (1.3 cm) single-fold bias tape; or fabric and ¾" (2 cm) bias tape maker.

• Glue stick.

Outdoor seat cushions
add color and comfort to
patio furniture. Above, a
custom pad is made to fit a
wooden bench. Right, a pad
is shaped to fit a resin chair.

HOW TO SEW A CHAIR OR BENCH PAD

1 Make a paper pattern of chair or bench seat to be covered by pad, rounding any sharp corners. Cut pattern; check fit. This pattern is used for cutting the fabric.

2 Trace pattern on separate piece of paper; mark cutting line ⅝" (1.5 cm) in from traced line. Cut pattern on inner marked line. This pattern is used for cutting the foam.

3 Cut the pad front and pad back from decorator fabric, using pattern for fabric. Place pattern for foam on the polyurethane foam; trace, using marking pen. Cut foam on marked line, using rotary cutter or scissors.

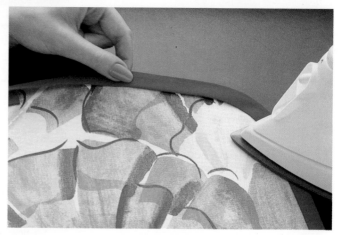

4 Make bias tape, opposite, if desired; or use purchased bias tape. Press bias tape into curved shape to match shape of pad. To prevent puckering, stretch tape slightly as you press.

5 Center foam on wrong side of pad back; place pad front over foam, right side up, matching raw edges of fabric. Pin layers together.

6 Machine-baste ¼" (6 mm) seam around pad, using zipper foot.

7 Apply small amount of glue stick to seam allowance of pad back. Finger-press wide side of bias tape into position, with raw edges of pad fabric at foldline of tape; overlap ends of tape about 1" (2.5 cm).

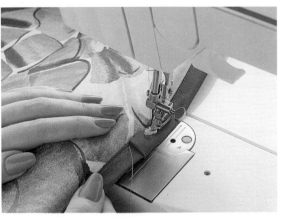

8 Turn pad over. Glue-baste the narrow side of the tape to the seam allowance of pad front, using small amount of glue stick. Join ends of the tape by folding under ¼" (6 mm) on overlapped end; glue-baste.

9 Stitch along inner edge of tape, using zipper foot, with narrow edge of tape facing up.

HOW TO MAKE BIAS TAPE USING A BIAS TAPE MAKER

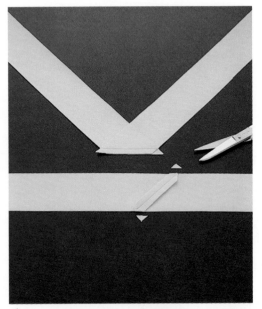

1 Fold fabric in half diagonally on the bias grain of fabric; cut along the fold. Cut bias strips, 1¾" (4.5 cm) wide.

2 Join strips, right sides together, by placing them at right angles, offset ¼" (6 mm); strips will form a "V." Stitch ¼" (6 mm) seam across the ends. Press seams open; trim seam allowances even with edges. Raw edges match on long edges after seams are stitched.

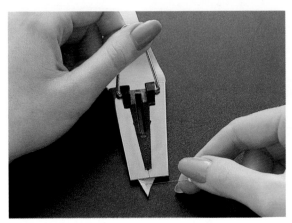

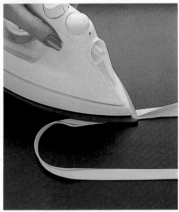

3 Thread pointed end of the bias strip through channel at wide end of tape maker, bringing point out at narrow end. Using pin, pull fabric through slot opening; pin the point of strip to pressing surface.

4 Press folded bias strip as you pull tape maker the length of the strip. Tape maker automatically folds raw edges to center of strip.

5 Fold bias tape lengthwise, with folded edge on bottom extending a scant ⅛" (3 mm) beyond folded edge of upper layer; press.

TREE TABLES

For a whimsical accent, build a side table designed to resemble a tree. An easy sponge painting technique produces a textured, decorative finish. This table is simple to construct; the only power saw necessary is a jigsaw.

The table is built using medium-density fiberboard, which is available with or without a veneer overlay. The veneer overlay is not necessary to make this project. Medium-density fiberboard, often referred to as MDF, is easy to work with and requires minimal sanding. MDF is usually stocked in 4' × 8' (1.27 × 2.48 m) sheets, measuring 49" × 96" (125 × 244 cm). Two tables can be cut from one sheet. Some lumber yards will cut sheets in half or to your specifications.

For easy construction and assembly, the base of the table is made in two sections, with cutout slots that allow the base sections to interlock. To make the table suitable for outdoor use, apply a marine spar varnish after the decorative painting is completed.

Because the varnish provides the protective finish, it is not necessary to paint the table using exterior-quality paint; however, these paints may be more resistant to fading. If the table will be used in a protected area, such as a porch or sun room, a clear acrylic or polyurethane finish can be used.

Select paint colors in at least three different shades or intensities each, for the foliage and the trunk. If you will be using a marine spar varnish, keep in mind that the amber tone of the varnish may affect the finished look of the table; you may want to test the varnish over your paint colors on a scrap piece of wood before painting the table.

The finished table measures about 24" (61 cm) in diameter and about 24½" (62.3 cm) in height.

Tree tables can be designed and painted for a variety of looks. Opposite, the table is painted to resemble an apple tree. Left, the table is painted with tones of peaches and greens.

MATERIALS

- Medium-density fiberboard or MDF, ½" (1.3 cm) thick; one 4' × 8' (1.27 × 2.48 m) sheet is enough for two tables.
- Four ¾" × 1⁵⁄₁₆" (2 × 3.3 cm) desk-top, or figure-8, fasteners with 8 × ½" (1.3 cm) flat-head screws.
- Jigsaw, with blade suitable for dense wood.
- Drill and ⅛" drill bit.
- Sandpaper; mechanical pencil.
- Paintbrush for applying primer and base coat.
- 2" (5 cm) piece of natural sea sponge.

- Primer.
- Latex or acrylic paint for base coat of trunk and foliage areas; two or more accent paints each for trunk and foliage, for sponge paint finish.
- Clear acrylic or polyurethane finish; use marine spar varnish if table will be used outdoors.

CUTTING DIRECTIONS

Cut from the fiberboard two 20" × 24" (51 × 61 cm) rectangles for the base pieces of the table. Cut one 24" (61 cm) square for the table top; set aside.

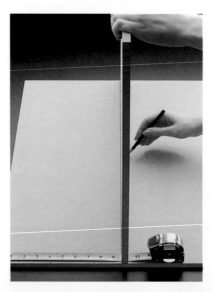

1 Mark line on base piece 9¾" (25 cm) from one long edge. Position and center the remaining base piece, on its side as shown, aligning the edge with the marked line. Using a mechanical pencil, mark thickness of the board for the cutout slot. Repeat for the remaining base piece.

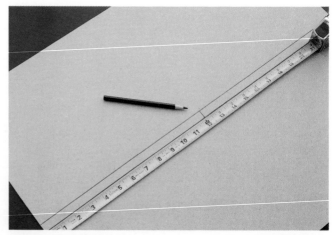

2 Mark a perpendicular line 12⅛" (30.8 cm) from the end of the board for length of cutout slot. Repeat for remaining base piece.

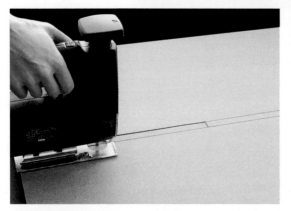

3 Cut, using a jigsaw and following marked line, from edge of board to perpendicular line; at end of cut, keep hand on jigsaw and shut blade off. Remove blade when movement has stopped. Repeat for remaining marked line.

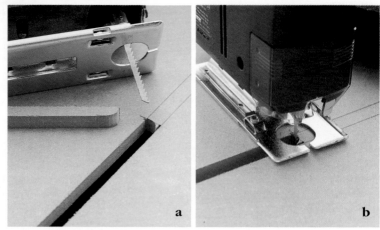

a **b**

4 Cut and remove center strip, making curved cut to one corner **(a).** Then trim end of slot even with marked line **(b).** (Marked line was extended for clarity.)

5 Repeat steps 3 and 4 for remaining base piece. Slide pieces together to check fit; mark a registration line as shown, for realigning pieces. Recut or sand the fiberboard as necessary, making sure to match registration line when rechecking fit. Pieces should fit snug but allow some ease for painted finish.

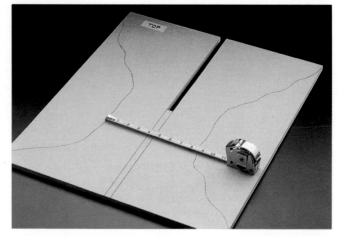

6 Label top of each base piece; cutout slot will be at bottom of one piece and at top of remaining piece. Mark one base piece with design of tree trunk, allowing at least 4" (10 cm) from outer edge of trunk to center of board.

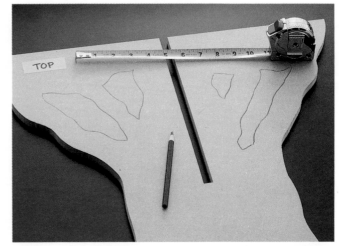

7 Cut about 1½" (3.8 cm) from marked lines to remove bulk of excess board; then recut, following marked lines. Mark and cut remaining base piece, using completed base as a pattern; match top ends of pieces.

8 Mark four cutout areas as shown to create tree branches on upper portion of one base; mark the cutout areas at least 1¾" (4.5 cm) from center slot and 1¼" (3.2 cm) from outside edge of base.

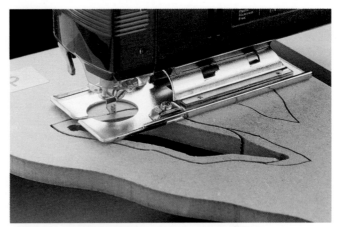

9 Drill a hole slightly larger than jigsaw blade about ¼" (6 mm) in from each end of area to be cut. Insert the jigsaw blade into drilled hole; cut about ¼" (6 mm) from the marked line to opposite drilled hole. Repeat along the opposite edge.

10 Make angled cut to marked line, starting at center area of cutout; cut to center of pointed or curved end. Repeat to cut opposite side. Continue to cut the remainder of cutout.

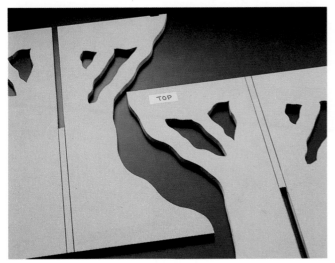

12 Mark and cut four notches for the desktop fasteners at upper edge of base pieces; position one notch about ¾" (2 cm) from each outside edge. Make the side cuts first; then cut as in step 4, opposite. Wide end of fastener should fit flush in the notch.

11 Mark cutout areas to create branches for remaining base piece; cut on marked lines.

(Continued)

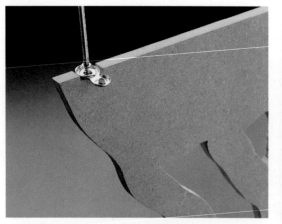

13 Position wide end of fastener, rounded side down, in notch; mark placement for the screw. Predrill, using a ⅛" drill bit; secure fastener. Repeat for remaining fasteners.

14 Mark two perpendicular lines, centered, on underside of tabletop. Mark a line ¼" (6 mm) from each side of the marked lines; outer lines mark placement for table base. Using a straightedge and pencil, mark a circle measuring 12" (30.5 cm) from center point.

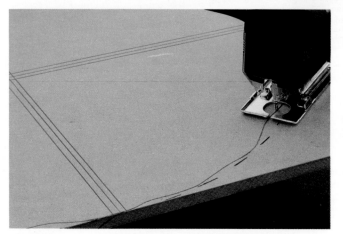

15 Mark a wavy design line for edge of the tabletop, using markings for circle as a guide; cut, following the design line.

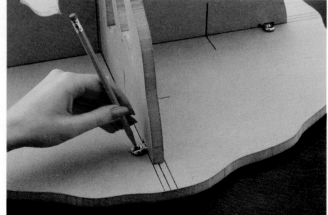

16 Position the table base, upside down, on underside of tabletop, aligning base with marked lines. Mark registration lines for realigning tabletop to base. Mark the placement for screws.

17 Predrill holes for screws on tabletop; to prevent drilling through tabletop, mark ⅜" (1 cm) depth on drill bit, using masking tape; drill until tape reaches surface of board.

18 Secure base to tabletop. Run hand over tabletop at screw locations; if the surface is raised, lightly sand until the surface is flush. Lightly sand the edges of tabletop, base, and cutouts in base. Disassemble the table; apply sponge paint finish (opposite), or paint table as desired.

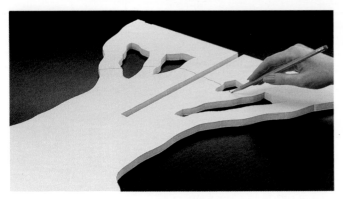

1 Apply primer; allow to dry. Apply second coat to edges of table. Using pencil, lightly mark design lines for lower edge of foliage on base pieces.

2 Apply base coats of paint to table base, using colors of medium value; allow to dry. Using damp natural sponge, dab sponge into darkest paint color for trunk; blot sponge lightly on paper towel. Press sponge repeatedly onto trunk area of table until individual sponge marks cannot be seen; apply more paint to sponge as necessary, blotting on paper towel.

3 Rinse sponge. Allow paint to dry. Apply remaining paint colors to trunk with sponge as in step 2, filling in between previous sponge marks to blend colors.

4 Repeat steps 2 and 3 to sponge paint the foliage on the tabletop and foliage area of base.

5 Apply marine spar varnish, clear acrylic finish, or polyurethane finish, following manufacturer's directions. Allow to dry thoroughly; assemble table.

FOUNTAINS

Bring the soothing sound of trickling water to a porch or patio with a fountain. Choose from a three-tier cascade fountain or a single-tier strawberry-pot fountain. Both styles are easily assembled using inexpensive terra-cotta pottery and are also suitable for indoor use.

A small, submersible pump recirculates the water in the fountain. This style pump is available at garden centers that carry supplies for ponds and at some aquarium stores. For best results, select a pump with a flow-rate adjuster. These pumps provide a range of flow rates, allowing you to adjust the water flow to prevent any splashing. Small clamps are also available for restricting the flow of water; attach one of these clamps to the plastic hose leading from the pump outlet. Refer to the operating instructions provided with the pump for specific instructions on adjusting the flow rate. When operating the pump outdoors, always connect it to a GFCI (ground-fault circuit interrupter) outdoor receptacle.

When selecting the terra-cotta pottery, look for pieces that are smooth and uniform. Make sure the pieces will rest together evenly by stacking them as they will be assembled in the fountain. To allow for the flow of water in the fountain, small openings must be cut in some of the pottery pieces. Because of the soft, porous nature of terra-cotta pottery, this is easily accomplished using a drill bit and a file. To make the fountain watertight, it is also necessary to seal the interior of the base container.

Check the water level in the fountains frequently. When they are operated

in dry weather, evaporation may require the water to be replenished every two or three days. The terra-cotta pots may develop a white residue; this can be removed using a nylon or natural-bristle brush. For a thorough cleaning, the fountains can be easily disassembled.

Submersible pump, *concealed inside an inverted pot, rests in the base container and recirculates the water. The electrical cord of the pump fits through a notch in the inverted pot and extends over the back edge of the base container. For best results, the base container should be deep enough to submerge the water intake portion of the pump.*

Fountains *are easily made from terra-cotta pottery. The strawberry-pot fountain (right) is topped with potted ivy. The three-tier fountain (opposite) is embellished with river stones and potted New Guinea impatiens.*

HOW TO MAKE A THREE-TIER FOUNTAIN

MATERIALS

GENERAL SUPPLIES

- Drill; 3/8" masonry drill bit; conical rotary rasp bit.
- 8" (20.5 cm) round bastard file.
- Small submersible pump, with flow rate of about 60 gal. (228 L) per hour.
- 12" (30.5 cm) length of flexible tubing, with diameter to fit discharge outlet of pump.
- Extra-thick aerosol clear acrylic sealer.
- Marine-grade sealant or adhesive.

FOR BASE OF FOUNTAIN

- One terra-cotta saucer, about 18" (46 cm) in diameter and 3" (7.5 cm) high.

FOR TALLEST COLUMN

- One 6" (15 cm) terra-cotta pot, 5" (12.5 cm) high; this pot conceals pump.
- One 8" (20.5 cm) terra-cotta saucer.
- One 4" (10 cm) terra-cotta saucer.

FOR MIDDLE COLUMN

- One 5" (12.5 cm) terra-cotta pot, 4" (10 cm) high.
- One 6" (15 cm) terra-cotta saucer.

FOR SHORTEST COLUMN:

- Two 4" (10 cm) terra-cotta saucers.

1 Apply masking tape around the upper outside edge of the saucer for the fountain base. Apply extra-thick aerosol sealer to the inside of saucer; repeat to apply two or three coats. This seals the interior of saucer.

2 Center and mark an X on the bottom of 8" (20.5 cm) saucer, using ruler and permanent-ink marker. Soak 8" (20.5 cm) saucer, 6" (15 cm) pot, 6" (15 cm) saucer, and two 4" (10 cm) saucers in water for at least one hour. Remove 8" (20.5 cm) saucer from the water.

3 Place 8" (20.5 cm) saucer on scrap piece of wood. Drill hole at marking, using 3/8" masonry drill bit. Enlarge hole, if necessary, using conical rasp bit, so the plastic tubing fits snugly through hole; drill slowly, applying light pressure, and check fit often.

4 File one notch for water spout in edge of 8" (20.5 cm) saucer, using round bastard file; angle file toward saucer as shown, so outer lip is higher than inner edge. This angle creates best water flow. Repeat to file one angled notch each in 6" (15 cm) saucer and 4" (10 cm) saucer.

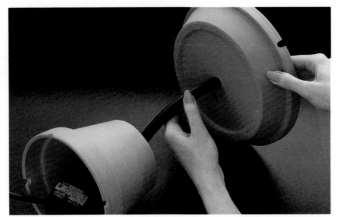

5 File four notches, equally spaced, in upper edge of 6" (15 cm) pot, filing one notch to accommodate electrical cord of pump; the angle of these notches is not critical to water flow. Repeat to file four notches in the remaining 4" (10 cm) saucer.

6 Connect tubing to discharge outlet of pump; if it is difficult to slide tubing over outlet, place end of tubing in hot water for one or two minutes. Insert opposite end of tubing through inverted 6" (15 cm) pot, then through 8" (20.5 cm) saucer as shown.

7 Position pump and stacked unit in base saucer; adjust cord to fit in notch of pot. Pull tubing taut; trim about ½" (1.3 cm) above saucer. Seal any gaps between tubing and saucer with bead of sealant; allow sealant to cure, following manufacturer's instructions.

8 Invert saucer with four notches, and center in larger saucer, concealing tubing. Stack middle column as shown, and place in base saucer. Place inverted, unnotched saucer in base saucer; place notched 4" (10 cm) saucer on top for short column.

10 Add embellishments, such as rocks, gravel, coral, or shells. Accent tallest column with potted plant, candle, or small statue; this weights down the notched, inverted saucer.

9 Fill base saucer with water, about ⅜" (1 cm) from rim; plug in pump. Adjust the position of notched saucers and the flow rate of pump as necessary.

HOW TO MAKE A STRAWBERRY-POT FOUNTAIN

MATERIALS

- General supplies as for three-tier fountain (page 100).

- Base container, such as decorative terra-cotta azalea pot, about 15" (38 cm) in diameter and about 4" (10 cm) deep.

- One terra-cotta azalea pot, about 10" (25.5 cm) in diameter, to fit inverted in base container; this pot conceals pump.

- One terra-cotta saucer, about 8" (20.5 cm) in diameter, to set on inverted pot.

- One terra-cotta strawberry pot, about 10" (25.5 cm) high.

- Plaster of Paris and duct tape or masking tape, for filling drainage hole of base container.

- Decorative rocks and gravel.

- Embellishment, such as potted plant for top of strawberry pot.

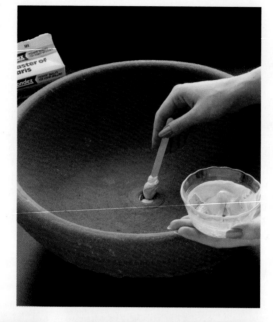

1 Fill any drainage hole of the base container, using plaster of Paris. To fill the hole, tape the bottom of the container with duct tape or masking tape. Mix a small amount of plaster of Paris, following the manufacturer's instructions. Partially fill the hole with plaster; allow to harden. Repeat to fill remainder of the hole. Seal interior of the bowl as on page 100, step 1.

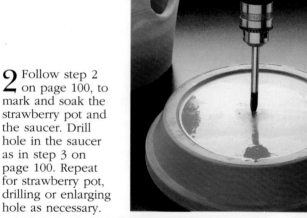

2 Follow step 2 on page 100, to mark and soak the strawberry pot and the saucer. Drill hole in the saucer as in step 3 on page 100. Repeat for strawberry pot, drilling or enlarging hole as necessary.

3 Soak the azalea pot in water for at least one hour. File four notches, equally spaced, in the upper edge of the pot, using a round bastard file; file one of the notches to accommodate electrical cord of pump.

4 Connect tubing to pump as in step 6 on page 101. Insert opposite end of tubing through inverted azalea pot, the saucer, and then through bottom of strawberry pot.

5 Position pump and stacked unit in base container; adjust the cord to fit through notch of pot. Pull tubing taut. Seal any gaps between tubing and strawberry pot with a bead of sealant; use stick or straw, if necessary. Allow the sealant to cure, following the manufacturer's instructions.

6 Fill strawberry pot with about 3" (7.5 cm) of gravel, keeping tubing centered. Trim tubing about ½" (1.3 cm) above gravel.

7 Fill the base saucer with water, about ⅜" (1 cm) from rim; plug in pump. Adjust flow rate of pump as necessary. Place rocks or shells, if desired, in rim of the saucer. Add other embellishments as desired, such as a potted plant on top of the strawberry pot.

MORE IDEAS FOR FOUNTAINS

Make a hole in saucer and pot to accommodate the stem of the fountain head; connect the fountain head to pump, using plastic tubing.

Mini-bell fountain head (above) is attached to a pump for a simple and decorative fountain. The fountain is made by placing an 11" (28 cm) saucer on top of a 7" (18 cm) inverted pot. A birdbath dish is used for the base of the container. The pump used in this fountain has a flow rate of 160 gal. (608 L) per hour.

Pump with fountain head attachment (right) is placed in a water garden (page 36). The pump used in this fountain has a flow rate of 80 gal. (304 L) per hour, creating a fountain spray about 10" (25.5 cm) high.

WIND CHIMES FROM FLATWARE

Hung in the breeze, wind chimes made from vintage flatware take on a unique musical quality. For ease in bending and drilling holes in the flatware, use silver or silver-plated flatware. Odd pieces of silver and silver-plated flatware can be found inexpensively at antique shops or thrift stores. To add to the charm of the wind chime, select flatware in a variety of patterns and use a variety of serving pieces.

HOW TO MAKE A WIND CHIME FROM FLATWARE

MATERIALS

- Vintage silver or silver-plated flatware: two dinner forks for top support and center chime; four smaller pieces, such as butter knives, small spoons, or dessert forks, for outer chimes.
- Drill and ¹⁄₁₆" drill bit; emery cloth.
- Needlenose pliers.
- Clear monofilament fishing line, 30-lb. (13.5 k) test.

1 Drill one hole in handle of each flatware piece, with hole centered and about ¼" (6 mm) from upper edge. Smooth rough edges around holes on back side of flatware, using an emery cloth.

2 Drill one hole in dinner fork for top of wind chime, with the hole centered and about ¼" (6 mm) above the tines. Smooth rough edges around holes on back side of fork, using an emery cloth.

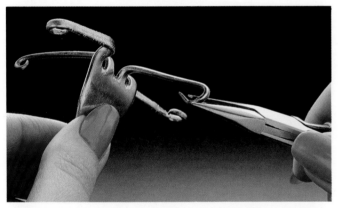

3 Bend tines of dinner fork for top support, using pliers, so tines extend in each direction as shown. Repeat for dinner fork for center chime. Bend and curl ends of each tine upward to form a loop.

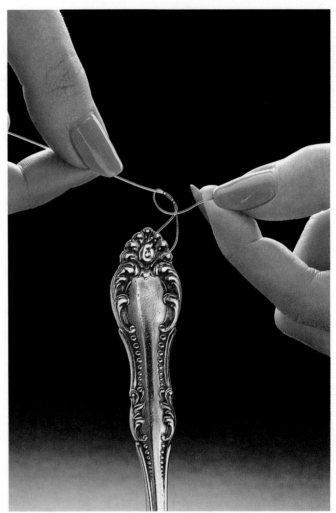

4 Insert fishing line through hole in fork for center chime; twist end around fishing line two times. Secure line by bringing end through loop; pull tight. Cut off excess line.

6 Tie and suspend flatware for one of the outer chimes from one tine loop of top support; adjust the length of fishing line so lower portion of the flatware strikes against bent tine of center chime. Repeat for remaining outer chimes.

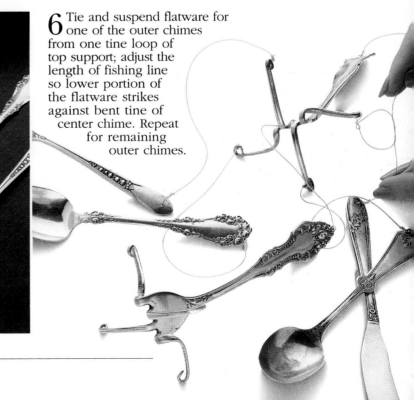

5 Repeat step 4 to tie the center chime to top support fork; the handle of the center chime should be about 5" (12.5 cm) below tines. Secure a loop for hanging through the hole in handle of the top support fork.

TWIG WREATHS

Use twigs to create a wreath with a textured, woodsy look. Change the embellishments for each season, using natural items gathered from your yard or walks in the woods. Or for longer-lasting displays, embellish a twig wreath with artificial or preserved foliage. Many embellishments can be simply tucked securely within the twigs, allowing you to use the same wreath year-round. Or make several wreaths, using a variety of twigs.

MATERIALS

- Twigs and small branches; pruning shears.
- Flat wire wreath base.
- 24-gauge paddle floral wire; wire cutter.
- Natural or artificial embellishments, such as pussy-willow stems and silk ivy for spring, artificial fruit and berries for summer, autumn leaves and dried pods for fall, and pine boughs and pinecones for winter.
- Ribbon or raffia, optional.

Spring wreath (opposite), made using birch twigs, features a watering can, seed packets, and artificial vegetables. Sheet moss is tucked between the twigs for additional color.

Autumn wreath (right) is made using branches from a winged euonymus bush. A potted cactus becomes the focal point, and dried chili peppers tucked into the wreath add color.

HOW TO MAKE
A TWIG WREATH

1 Cut twigs into lengths ranging from 10" to 13" (25.5 to 33 cm) long. Bundle several twigs together; wrap with paddle floral wire. Secure paddle floral wire to the wire wreath base. Place twig bundle on base, and tightly wrap with floral wire to secure.

3 Add seasonal embellishments; tuck items between twigs, securing with wire, if necessary.

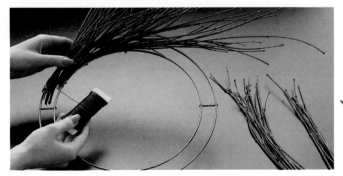

2 Secure additional twig bundles to base, until entire base is covered; angle bundles so the twigs radiate out in one direction and cover wire of previous bundles.

WREATHS WITH RIBBON STREAMERS

A wreath embellished with ribbons adds a festive display of color on the patio or at the front entrance of your home. With the wreath hung horizontally under the eaves of the house, the ribbon streamers can blow in the breeze.

MATERIALS

- 15" to 20" (38 to 51 cm) grapevine or twig wreath.
- Craft ribbons, 1½" to 2" (3.8 to 5 cm) wide, in assorted colors.
- Wire plant hanger.
- Wall bracket or ceiling hook.

CUTTING DIRECTIONS

Cut ribbons for streamers and bows about 45" (115 cm) long, cutting ends diagonally; you will need one streamer and one bow of the same color at each location, spaced about 6" (15 cm) apart around the wreath.

HOW TO MAKE WREATHS WITH RIBBON STREAMERS

1 Tie one end of a streamer ribbon around a few grapevines or twigs on bottom of wreath. Repeat for remaining streamers, spacing them about 6" (15 cm) apart around wreath and distributing colors as desired.

2 Insert one of the bow ribbons under a few twigs or grapevines at top of wreath, positioning it directly above a streamer of the same color; pull through about one-half the length of the ribbon. Knot the ribbon to secure it to wreath.

3 Tie ribbon into bow. Repeat step 2 for remaining ribbons, and tie bows.

4 Attach wire plant hanger to top of wreath, with the wires spaced evenly around wreath; twist wire ends around grapevine or twigs. Hang the wreath from wall bracket or ceiling hook.

MORE IDEAS FOR DECORATING WITH RIBBONS

Easter tree *(left) is decorated with pastel bows and plastic eggs for a cheerful effect.*

Evergreen *(opposite) is decorated with large red bows and string lighting for Christmas.*

Ribbons and jingle bells *(opposite) make this miniwreath a clever outdoor decoration for Christmas. A variation of the wreath on page 108, this wreath is embellished using many narrow ribbons, with a bell tied at the end of each streamer.*

Woven ribbon placemats *(below) add a colorful accent to a party table. After weaving the ribbons, stitch them together around the outer rows.*

*Creative
Lighting Effects*

STRING LIGHTING

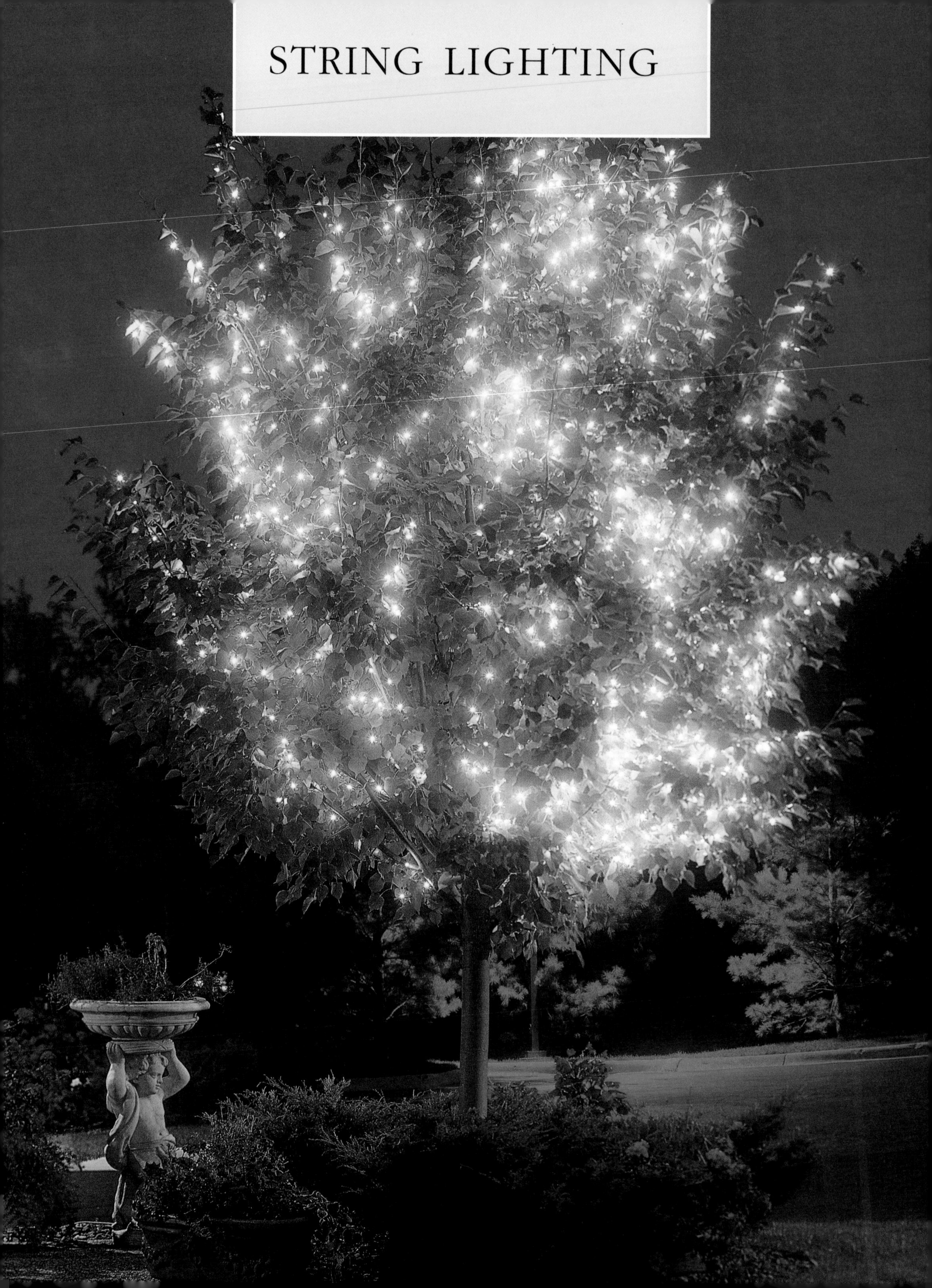

The glow of lights on trees and bushes extends a cheerful greeting and brings a festive sparkle outside. While colored lights are popular during the Christmas season, miniature white garden lights can add a captivating glow for any occasion. Unless the foliage is very dense, many trees and bushes can be successfully lit any time of the year.

For impact, decorate trees and bushes lavishly with lights. A single well-lit tree will have more impact than several sparsely lit trees. In general, use one hundred lights per foot (30.5 cm) of tree height or diameter of tree canopy. To add depth to the display, string the lights in a zigzag fashion, from the trunk area out toward the branches.

When stringing lights, it is important to use an outdoor-rated, three-prong extension cord and ground-fault circuit interrupter (GFCI) outdoor receptacle or outlet. Never use more light wattage than the rating of the extension cord and electrical circuit.

Lighting packages will indicate the total light wattage and how many light strings can be safely connected together. Most standard outdoor-rated miniature lights can be plugged end to end in units up to three hundred lights. Multiple units can be plugged into an extension cord with two or three power outlets, provided the total light wattage does not exceed the watts rating of the extension cord.

TIPS FOR STRING LIGHTING

Work with lights plugged in; this will help ensure that lights are distributed evenly.

Select high-quality lights with locking devices for bulbs.

Work with light strand draped over shoulder.

Replace burned-out bulbs and plug fuses immediately to prevent strain on remaining bulbs and light strings.

Make extension pole for stringing lights in difficult-to-reach areas. Drill hole in end of wooden pole, such as a dowel. Bend a length of coat-hanger wire as shown, using pliers; insert wire ends of hanger into hole at end of dowel. Secure wire to wooden pole, using duct tape.

String lighting adds a festive touch to outdoor settings. Above, string lights are used on an evergreen tree. Opposite, string lights add drama to a deciduous tree.

HOW TO STRING LIGHTS ON TREES & SHRUBS

MATERIALS

- Outdoor-rated extension cord.
- Weatherproof miniature lights.
- Brown duct tape.
- Vinyl-wrapped wire.

1 Secure plug end of extension cord to trunk of tree, using duct tape; position plug near base of limbs for ball-style tree or near middle of trunk for evergreen tree. Plug cord into outdoor-rated circuit receptacle. Plug first string of lights into outlet; secure near the trunk, using vinyl-wrapped wire, or wrap light strand around nearby twig or branch.

2 Extend lights down length of branch; wrap strand once or twice around tip of branch to secure; keep wire of lights taut.

3 Extend lights back down length of same branch; secure with vinyl-wrapped wire or by wrapping light strand around twig or small branch. Secure light strand near the base of adjacent branch.

4 Continue to string the lights around branches of the tree, using additional strings of lights as desired and taking care not to exceed manufacturer's recommendations for connecting light sets together. In difficult-to-reach areas, use extension pole (page 115) to position the lights.

Paper shades, *cut from decorative paper, are wrapped around cool-burning bulbs on a string of lights for a lantern effect.*

HOW TO MAKE PAPER SHADES

1 Make pattern by folding square of paper in half lengthwise, then crosswise. Mark an arc about 3" (7.5 cm) from folded corner; mark a second arc ¼" (6 mm) from corner. Cut on the marked lines; trim away one-quarter of circle.

2 Cut shades from decorative paper, using pattern. Wrap paper around light; secure with tape or staple.

LANDSCAPE LIGHTING

Low-voltage lighting systems provide safe, easy-to-install lighting for functional applications and decorative effects. Available in do-it-yourself kits, the lights are powered with a transformer and cables that are buried 4" to 6" (10 to 15 cm) in the ground. The transformer plugs into an outdoor outlet and reduces the normal 120-volt house current to a safe 12-volt level. The spike-mounted fixtures are snapped in place along the cable where desired. Install lighting systems following the manufacturer's directions.

Low-voltage floodlights (right) highlight a distinctive tree. (Photo courtesy of Bachman's Landscaping Service; Sue Hartley, photography.)

Path lighting (below), installed with a low-voltage light system, illuminates a walkway at the front entrance of the home. (Photo courtesy of Toro News Center.)

Arbor (above) is highlighted with string lighting.

Grapevine wreath (left) is wrapped with lights for a dazzling window accent. Position the cord in an inconspicuous location to the side of the wreath.

CREATIVE LIGHTING EFFECTS

ICE LUMINARIES

In cold-weather climates, the glow of ice luminaries adds a warm glow to dark winter nights. To create this lighting effect, simply place a candle into a well in a large block of ice. Use ice luminaries to line driveways and walkways. Or, add interest to a backyard view by clustering several on a patio or deck.

Ice luminaries can be used as long as the temperature remains below the freezing point. Brush the snow off the candles periodically and spray the ice formation

with water to return the ice to its clear state. For long-burning luminaries, use pillar candles.

MATERIALS

- Plastic bucket, such as a one-gallon ice cream container.
- Plastic jar, such as a peanut butter or mayonnaise jar.
- Votive or pillar candle.

Large planters can be put to good use in the winter by making holiday arrangements using ice luminaries and sprigs of evergreen and berries.

HOW TO MAKE AN ICE LUMINARY

1 Ice cream buckets. Center jar in the bucket; place rocks in the jar to weight it. Fill the bucket with water, up to the rim of jar. Place the bucket outdoors or in the freezer until the water is frozen. Remove the rocks from the jar.

2 Pour warm water into jar to release it from ice; remove jar.

3 Wrap the bucket with warm, wet towel to release ice from bucket. Place candle into the well in the ice.

Deep buckets. Fill bucket partway with water; surface of water should be below rim of the bucket a distance greater than height of candle you will use for well in the ice. Freeze water. Complete luminary, following steps 1 to 3, above, centering jar on top of ice in step 1.

DECOUPAGE GLASS LUMINARIES

Rose bowl luminaries (above) line a deck rail for a festive look at an outdoor party. A votive, placed in the center of a large bowl, is used as a centerpiece on a buffet table.

Fish bowls (left), attractively embellished with handmade paper, sit on each side of the front door, welcoming guests.

Decorative luminaries can be made from glass containers by gluing pieces of tissue paper to the outside surface. When the candles are lit, the light softly glows through the paper. These luminaries can be made in any size, depending on the size of the container selected.

Colored tissue paper, including matte-finished and pearlized, is available from most card and stationery shops. For a wide color selection, you may want to select paper at an art supply store. Translucent decorative papers can also be used.

To prevent the luminaries from fading, avoid exposing them to direct sunlight.

MATERIALS

- Glass container.
- Tissue paper or translucent decorative paper.
- Decoupage medium; brush or sponge applicator.
- Aerosol acrylic sealer.
- Pillar or votive candle.

HOW TO MAKE DECOUPAGE GLASS LUMINARIES

1 Cut the tissue paper into small pieces, varying shapes and sizes as desired. Apply a thin layer of decoupage medium to one piece of paper, using sponge applicator.

2 Position paper on outside of container; gently smooth in place, using finger. Continue applying pieces of paper randomly, overlapping them as desired, until the container is covered. Wrap paper around upper edge of container, to cover rim on inside.

3 Cut decorative motifs, such as geometric shapes or flowers, from paper, if desired, and apply them with decoupage medium.

4 Apply light coat of aerosol acrylic sealer; allow sealer to dry. Apply second coat. Place pillar or votive candle in center of container.

MORE IDEAS FOR LUMINARIES

Sheets of Mylar® (above), wrapped around a votive container, add a shimmery effect.

Minnow buckets (left) become decorative luminaries when illuminated with candles.

Tree branches (above) are drilled and fitted with votive candles for a rustic look. Clamp the log horizontally and drill an opening the depth of the votive, using a spade drill bit. To prevent fire hazard, trim outer layers of bark away from hole.

Sand-filled terra-cotta planters (opposite), filled with pillar candles, illuminate the outdoors. Hurricane pots are made by placing glass chimneys in the sand-filled pots.

INDEX

CREDITS

President: Iain Macfarlane

OUTDOOR DECOR
Created by: The Editors of
   Creative Publishing international, Inc.

Books available in this series:
Bedroom Decorating, Creative Window Treatments, Decorating for Christmas, Decorating the Living Room, Creative Accessories for the Home, Decorating with Silk & Dried Flowers, Kitchen & Bathroom Ideas, Decorating the Kitchen, Decorative Painting, Decorating Your Home for Christmas, Decorating for Dining & Entertaining, Decorating with Fabric & Wallcovering, Decorating the Bathroom, Decorating with Great Finds, Affordable Decorating, Picture-Perfect Walls, More Creative Window Treatments, Outdoor Decor, The Gift of Christmas, Home Accents in a Flash, Painted Illusions, Halloween Decorating

Group Executive Editor: Zoe A. Graul
Editorial Manager: Dawn M. Anderson
Senior Editor: Rita C. Arndt
Project Manager: Elaine Johnson
Associate Creative Director:
   Lisa Rosenthal
Art Director: Mark Jacobson

Writers: Rita C. Arndt, Lori Ritter
Editor: Janice Cauley
Researcher/Designer: Michael Basler
Researchers: Linda Neubauer, Lori Ritter
Sample Production Manager:
   Carol Olson
Senior Technical Photo Stylist:
   Bridget Haugh
Technical Photo Stylists: Sue Jorgensen,
   Linda Neubauer, Nancy Sundeen
Styling Director: Bobbette Destiche
Project Stylists: Coralie Sathre,
   Joanne Wawra
Prop Stylist: Michele Joy
Prop Assistant/Shopper: Margo Morris
Lead Artisan: Carol Pilot
Artisans: Arlene Dohrman, Sharon
   Eklund, Phyllis Galbraith, Valerie Hill,
   Kristi Kuhnau, Virginia Mateen, Carol
   Pilot, Michelle Skudlarek, Nancy
   Sundeen, Marilu Theodor
*Vice President of Development Planning
   & Production:* Jim Bindas
Director of Photography: Mike Parker
Creative Photo Coordinator:
   Cathleen Shannon
Studio Manager: Marcia Chambers
Lead Photographer: Charles Nields
Photographers: Rebecca Hawthorne,
   Rex Irmen, Billy Lindner, Mark
   Macemon, Greg Wallace
Contributing Photographers:
   Phil Aarrestad, Doug Cummelin,
   Doug Deutscher, Mark Hardy, Chris
   Kausch, Steve Smith
Print Production Manager: Patt Sizer
Senior Desktop Publishing Specialist:
   Joe Fahey
Desktop Publishing Specialist:

Laurie Kristensen
Production Staff: Deborah Eagle,
   Kevin Hedden, Tom Hoops,
   Jeanette Moss, Mike Schauer,
   Greg Wallace, Kay Wethern
Shop Supervisor: Phil Juntti
Scenic Carpenters: Jon Hegge,
   Troy Johnson, Rob Johnstone,
   John Nadeau
Consultants: Ray Arndt, Sr., Sally Blohm,
   Connie Erickson, Patrick Kartes,
   Roger Lillemo, Meg Nordlie, Ossian Or,
   Lindsey Peterson, Mary Rosendahl
Contributors: Dritz Corporation; Dundee
   Garden Center; Offray Ribbon; Plaid
   Enterprises, Inc.; Walnut Hollow; Water
   Lilies by Forsman (Soni Forsman);
   Waverly, Division of F. Schumacher &
   Company
Sources for Product Information:
   Copper Verdigris Solution/Patina Green,
   pp. 46-47—MODERN OPTIONS, 2325
   3rd Street, #339, San Francisco, CA
   94107, (415) 252-5580
Printed on American paper by:
   R.R. Donnelley & Sons Co.

02 01 00 99   / 10 9 8 7

Creative Publishing international, Inc.
offers a variety of how-to books. For
information write:
   Creative Publishing international, Inc.
   Subscriber Books
   5900 Green Oak Drive
   Minnetonka, MN 55343